The
Pilgrim's Progress
Study Guide

The Pilgrim's Progress Study Guide

MAUREEN L. BRADLEY

P U B L I S H I N G
P.O. BOX 817 • PHILLIPSBURG • NEW JERSEY 08865

Unless otherwise indicated, Scripture quotations are from the New Ameri-
can Standard Bible. Copyright by the Lockman Foundation 1960, 1962,
1963, 1968, 1971, 1973, 1975, 1977.

Excerpts from The Pilgrim's Progress are from the 1985 edition published by
Barbour and Company, Inc., Uhrichsville, Ohio.

Printed in the United States of America

Library of Congress Cataloging-in-Publication Data

Bradley, Maureen L., 1948—
    The Pilgrim's progress study guide / Maureen L. Bradley.
       p.   cm.
    ISBN 0-87552-108-8
    1. Bunyan, John, 1628–1688. Pilgrim's progress. 2. Christian fiction,
English—Outlines, syllabi, etc. 3. Bible—In literature—Outlines, syllabi,
etc. I. Title.
PR3330.A95B73 1994
823'.4—dc20   94–12313

Contents

Preface

Some people learn to swim by jumping into the deep end of the pool—the sink-or-swim approach. This method has proved successful for many readers of classics such as *Pilgrim's Progress*. But Bunyan's allegorical style and older English have produced their share of "sinkers" as well—people who, for difficulty of staying afloat, miss the beauty and wisdom captured in Bunyan's allegory.

This study guide is designed to help readers understand, enjoy, and profit from Bunyan's timeless classic. In addition to providing background information on Bunyan himself and the writing of *Pilgrim's Progress*, it includes questions for review, discussion, and reflection on each of eleven lessons. Readers come face to face not only with the obstacles confronting Pilgrim but also with manifestations of the same challenges or temptations today. Each lesson concludes with a summary and applications of the truths discovered along the way, including insights from spiritual giants such as Charles Spurgeon, Alexander Whyte, George Cheever, Thomas Scott, and Thomas Shepard. The goal is to help readers learn and grow along with Pilgrim on his exciting adventure.

This study guide can be used as a companion to any number of editions of *Pilgrim's Progress*. At the beginning of each lesson there is a key to several popular editions, identifying the pages from each covered in that lesson. For example, lesson 1 covers pages 1–20 in the Barbour edition, pages 5–26 in the Moody Classic edition, pages 1–17 in the Revell Spire Book edition, and so on. Users of editions not shown in the key can also find the relevant pages for each lesson with little effort.

I would like to express my gratitude to the teaching ministry of Christ Presbyterian Church (PCA), Richmond, Indiana; to Mark Herzer for introducing me to and instructing me about the Puritans; to Elaine

Preface

Nelson of Inter-library Loan, Eli Lilly Library, Earlham College, for enabling me to obtain many out-of-print books needed in the preparation of this study manual; and to God for his graciousness in giving me a Christian family.

Introduction

to Pilgrim's Progress and Its Author, John Bunyan

The Book

What is it about The Pilgrim's Progress that has made it one of the best-selling books in history, second only to the Bible in sales? If we consider the success of literature to be in its influence over people, then Bunyan's book will possess such influence as long as the process of human redemption from sin is something angels or men desire to look into. Theologians of the past such as Augustine, Calvin, and Edwards have been recognized for their excellent theological teachings and writings, yet in the simple adventures of Christian (the main character of The Pilgrim's Progress) these same great theological truths are made to come to life before our very eyes. Bunyan turns theology and doctrine into an exciting adventure, and imaginations are captured as these truths are personified. A person who thoroughly understands The Pilgrim's Progress is an accomplished theologian. The peculiar power of this book is found in its presentation of truth reinforced by Scripture and common sense. If truth is the food of the human soul, then one is well fed by this book. Biblical truths come blasting through these pages like smart bombs hitting their targets of the mind and the heart. The great knowledge of the Bible that Bunyan possessed was attested to by Charles Spurgeon when he said, "Prick John Bunyan and he will bleed Bible" (Pictures from Pilgrim's Progress, p. 6). Spurgeon also related that outside of the Bible, Pilgrim's Progress was the most important book in his life and this statement is verified by the fact that he read Pilgrim's Progress at least one hundred times (twice a year).

Certainly some of Bunyan's own life experiences enter into *Pilgrim's Progress*, but does not this story reflect the journey of all true Christians? The story is told as an allegory. *Webster's Eighth New Collegiate Dictionary* defines allegory as "the expression by means of symbolic fictional figures and actions of truths or generalizations about human existence or experience." Thus, in *Pilgrim's Progress* the characters and places illustrate many of the inner struggles through which a Christian wrestles in this life. To briefly summarize the story, it is one man's realization of the fact that his soul is bound for hell and his subsequent seeking after Christ in spite of Satan's attempts to stop him. The man is saved as he comes to the cross of Christ. After his conversion he has many experiences and several encounters with Satan and his friends as he journeys towards heaven. We see how God provides for every need and is a sure help in every trial and temptation. The story ends with the pilgrim's entrance into heaven.

Rev. John Gulliver has described *Pilgrim's Progress* as follows:

> The opening scene gives vividly a contrast between justification by faith and by works, which is equal in polemic power to a dozen controversial treatises. In the progress of the allegory all the great doctrines, from total depravity to the resurrection, are clearly set forth, with the omission of scarcely a shade or a phase which has any practical adaptation or value. The reader is constantly stimulated by new discoveries. He adds, from each page, something to his store of thought on the profoundest and mightiest themes which can engage the human mind. He is not only entertained, but he is conscious of being instructed. (*The Complete Works of John Bunyan*, p. 6)

There are many books available to be read, but very few are worth reading, and they are those which stimulate imagination and thoughtful, godly meditation. This is such a book.

The Author

John Bunyan was born in Elstow, England, in 1628. He was from a poor family, his father being a tinker (one who makes and repairs pans and kettles), and he had limited opportunity for education. In his early life Bunyan had as much success in his wickedness as years later he had in his activities for the kingdom of God. A more detailed account of Bunyan's life may be had by reading his autobiography *Grace Abounding to the Chief of Sinners*. His spiritual life seems to have begun around the age of twenty-five. It was then that he first "looked unto Christ." He was baptized and joined a Baptist church. Three years later he was encouraged to preach at this same church. Bunyan preached for six years before he was arrested and placed in prison for not conforming to worship as prescribed by the Church of England and for preaching the gospel without a license. While in prison, he penned *Pilgrim's Progress*. The plentiful harvest this book has sown was brought into the kingdom of God by the anguish and tears of twelve years in a prison cell. We are able to see the godly, devout character of his heart during his prison years as we read some of his thoughts expressed in the poem "Prison Meditations":

> My feet upon Mount Zion stand, in that take thou delight.
> I am indeed in prison now in body, but my mind
> Is free to study Christ, and how unto me he is kind.
> For tho' men keep my outward man within their locks and
>   bars,
> Yet by the faith of Christ I can mount higher than the stars.
> Their fetters cannot spirits tame, nor tie up God from me;
> My faith and hope they cannot lame; above them I shall be.
> (Gulliver, *Works of John Bunyan*, p. 691)

What a source of strength and comfort his Bible (one of the two books he had while in prison, the other being *Foxe's Book of Martyrs*) must have been to him!

Upon being released from prison, he continued writing and became the pastor of a church in Bedford. Soon crowds were hanging entranced upon the words of Bunyan, for he was able to scoop up heaven and bring it down to the people. Through his preaching as well as his writing, Bunyan had the ability both to inform the intellect and to move the heart. Doctrinal truths were always communicated, for he understood that if the feelings are to be moved or the will is to be determined, it is always by means of truths settled in the intellect. But these truths were not allowed to lie dormant in the mind; they were ushered to the heart by a quickened conscience, and they lovingly caressed the will into action. Bunyan preached "with such divine unction and power, that John Owen, who heard him, made answer to Charles II, when the king ridiculed him for hearing an illiterate tinker, 'Please your majesty, could I possess that tinker's abilities for preaching, I would most gladly relinquish all my learning.' With all the learning of Owen, it would have been a good exchange" (Cheever, *Lectures on the Pilgrim's Progress*, p. 192). Because he was a master at personifying scriptural truths, his words, whether written or spoken, were instruments by which one person moves another closer to God. One who reads *The Complete Works of John Bunyan*, finds that they bear witness to the fact that Bunyan was a man in constant communion with God.

The Rev. George Cheever relates the following about Bunyan's death:

> It was in the successful prosecution of a labor of love and charity that he died: having traveled to Reading to make peace between an alienated son and father. The gentle spirit of Bunyan prevailed to do away the alienation; but for himself, returning to London on horseback through the rain, he fell sick with a mortal fever and died. On his dying bed he comforted those that wept about him, exhorting them to trust in God, and pray to Him for mercy and forgiveness of their sins, telling them what a glorious exchange it would be, to leave their troubles and cares of a wretched mortality, to live with Christ forever, with peace and joy inexpressible; expounding to them the comfortable scriptures by which they were to hope and assuredly come unto a blessed resurrection in the last day. He desired some to pray with him, and he joined with them in prayer: and his last words were these, "Weep not for me, but for yourselves. I go to the Father of our Lord Jesus Christ, who will, through the mediation of his blessed Son, receive me, though a sinner, where I hope we ere long shall meet to sing the new song, and remain everlastingly happy, world without end." (*Lectures*, p. 194)

Hence, John Bunyan died in 1688 at the age of sixty, having been one of those violent men who take the kingdom by force (Matthew 11:12).

1

Christian Stumbles

Barbour and Company, Inc. 1985, pp. 1–20
Discovery House *New Pilgrim's Progress* with notes, pp. 11–32
Moody *Pilgrim's Progress in Today's English*, pp. 11–26
Moody Classic Edition, pp. 5–26
Revell Spire Book, pp. 1–17
Whitaker House 1981 Edition, pp. 5–24

Questions for Discussion or Reflection

The first sentence of *Pilgrim's Progress* gives us the setting in which it was written. The den refers to the jail in which Bunyan was confined for preaching the gospel as a nonconformist. Though he was restrained by man from preaching the gospel from his pulpit, God was pleased to cause "the wrath of man to praise him" by Bunyan's writings while confined. Also keep in mind that as soon as Bunyan introduces a new character, we feel as if we already know him, so exactly is the new person's nature revealed by his name. In this first lesson we will meet characters such as Pliable and Obstinate. Christian is sidetracked for a while by Mr. Worldly Wiseman, whose enmity against the gospel is seen in the bad advice he gives to Christian. Christian is graciously rescued from his unhappy dilemma by a character named Evangelist. Let us now step into Bunyan's dream and commence our own adventure with the pilgrim on his journey.

1. We find the main character of the book dwelling in the City of Destruction. George Cheever makes these comments: "The City of Destruction! We are all inhabitants of it; no man needs ask, Where is it?

What is it? Who are its people? Alas! our world of sin is the City of Destruction, and we know of a certainty from God's Word that it is to be burned up, and that if we do not escape from it, though we may die at peace in it before its conflagration, yet to be found with its spirit in our souls when we die, is to be forever miserable" (*Lectures on the Pilgrim's Progress*, p. 217). What is the spirit of this world, which if found in our souls at death will bring us misery forever? Be specific and elaborate.

2. The "man clothed with rags" was able to know that there is a Creator from natural revelation, but an understanding of who God is and of his plan of salvation could only be found in the book the man was holding. What do you think was the name of the book he was reading? Why was this book so necessary?

3. What does the burden on his back represent? (See Psalm 38:4; Isaiah 64:6; Hebrews 2:2.)

4. When Graceless (the man clothed with rags; we will learn later in the narrative that this was the name he was known by when he lived in the City of Destruction) shared his distress with his wife and children, what was their reaction?

Have you ever observed that when the gospel is shared, either people are convicted or the gospel has the opposite effect and they are hardened?

5. Evangelist represents a preacher of the gospel of grace whom Christ has sent to ease the distress of the man. When Evangelist asked Graceless why he was crying, how did Graceless respond?

6. In his response to Evangelist's question, "Why not willing to die, since this life is attended with so many evils?" the man shows himself to be under the conviction of the Spirit of God as he feels the insupportable burden of sin upon his back and the dread of God's wrath against sin. Do you believe that these two elements are often absent in today's presentations of the gospel in evangelistic efforts? Explain.

7. According to Isaiah 30:33, what is Tophet?

8. When Graceless asks Evangelist, "Whither must I fly?" what is Evangelist's response?

9. What do you believe the "shining light" represents? (See Psalm 119:105; 2 Peter 1:19; John 3:3.)

Note: The name of the man clothed with rags (Graceless) is now changed to Christian.

10. Two neighbors, Obstinate and Pliable, "resolved to fetch Christian back by force." What is more important to Obstinate than leaving the City of Destruction? What is Obstinate's opinion of Christian's book?

A pliable person is a moldable type of individual, easily persuaded to believe whomever he is associated with at the time. He may yield to one opinion for a time but is easily induced to take up another. He is caught up in promises and hopes but does not count the cost of the journey. He has no perseverance. How did the character Pliable in *Pilgrim's Progress* exhibit these characteristics?

Note: Pliable had no burden (conviction of sin) on his back.

11. What does the Slough of Despond represent?

12. Help rescues Christian from the Slough of Despond. Who is he?

13. What do the "steps" represent, which Christian could have used to keep from going into the Slough of Despond?

14. It was not the pleasure of the King that the Slough remain. What measures had been taken to fix the situation, and what do these measures signify?

Why do you think the Slough could still not be mended even after all these efforts?

15. When Pliable arrived at home, what kind of reception did his neighbors give him? Have you ever seen an example of this type of behavior?

16. As Christian moves forward on his journey he meets a Mr. Worldly Wiseman from the town of Carnal Policy. What belief system do this man and the town he is from represent?

17. What was the first bit of advice Mr. Worldly Wiseman gave to Christian? Do you see this same advice being given today? Explain.

18. Mr. Worldly Wiseman does not like the fact that Christian was reading the Bible. To what place and to whom does he direct Christian? What erroneous view of salvation does this represent?

19. Regrettably, Christian follows Mr. Worldly Wiseman's directions and heads toward Mr. Legality's house. Where is it located and what are the consequences of Christian's choice?

This way is one that many have traveled and that many continue to go on. Why?

20. Evangelist finds Christian under Mount Sinai and looks severely upon him. He rebukes Christian for trying works salvation and becoming involved in a legalistic spirit. Against what three things does Evangelist warn Christian about Mr. Worldly Wiseman?

21. The Christian life cannot be enjoyed until the soul is convinced of the evil of legalism and rejects it. Any dependence on our own merit or works is error. We must wholly rely on Christ's active and passive obedience for our right standing with God. Do you agree? Why or why not?

Summary and Applications

We all live in the City of Destruction, and it is amazing that many people refuse to think about the most certain reality in human experience—death. Only ignorance of the Scriptures can enable people to rest securely when their immortal souls are in a gravely dangerous condition. Though the perils of the journey from the city that is doomed to the city of Immanuel are great, with conflicts and trials along the way, a soul with a conviction of sin and the recognition of its desperate wickedness will venture all, rather than stay where there is certain condemnation and misery. An individual's inherent desire for happiness and dread of pain become strong motives for such a pilgrimage. Thus, our man clothed with rags recognizes the necessity of fleeing from the wrath to come.

Many pilgrims are sidetracked or derailed by this world of sin in which we live. And to let the spirit of this world into our souls is to court certain disaster. We are given an excellent description of this spirit later in the book, at Vanity Fair. First John 2:15–16 also shows us the essence of this spirit when it mentions the lust of the flesh (gratifying our fleshly appetites in an intemperate manner by such activities as gluttony, drunkenness, and sexual immorality), the lust of the eyes (covetousness, greed, and an excessive attraction to the things of this world, such as cars, land, houses), and the pride of life (a seeking after fame and honor; self-adulation). There is much need for pilgrims to examine their lives daily by the light of the Scriptures to see if there is any part of the spirit of this world hiding in their hearts.

The necessity of the Bible is seen when the man clothed in rags opens the book and reads therein, which causes him to weep and tremble. All of creation points to the existence of a Creator, but an understanding of who he is and of his plan of salvation can only be gained through the special revelation contained in the Bible. Without the written Word to show us an absolute standard of right and wrong, we are lost in a sea of relativism. The Bible gives us an accurate description of God's character, his holiness, justice, grace, mercy, and so on. Without this accurate description people are prone to the most wicked idolatry in devising their own gods from their own imaginations, gods that are always far short of God's perfect character. And how able the Scriptures are to show us who we really are—enemies of God deserving his wrath, and all of us under sin (Romans 3:10–19)! If we do not have a burden of conviction of sin on our backs, one look at the Bible's description of the human heart should give us one (Jeremiah 17:9).

The man then shares his distress with his wife and children. Their reaction, sad to say, is indeed the reaction of the majority of the people in this world—"they began to be hardened." People achieve this hardness of heart and try to quiet their minds with a false peace by many diversions (sports, entertainment, materialism, etc.) and the absence of serious books and friends from their lives. However, for those who have seen from Scripture by the influence of the Holy Spirit that they are condemned to die and subject to the judgment to come, no such attempts to quiet the soul will work.

Though the Scriptures are sufficient to make us wise unto salvation, the Lord sends Evangelist, a minister of the gospel, to help explain more fully the way of salvation. We note that Evangelist does not try to persuade the man that his fears are groundless by presenting a view of God that is unbalanced, a view that presents the love and mercy of God but leaves out his holiness and justice (Exodus 34:7). This incorrect presentation of the gospel is very prevalent today. An even worse presentation includes the idea that good self-esteem is a cure for our distress, whereas this will only lead us into a false and fatal security. Evangelist points the man to Christ through continued Bible reading with the Holy Spirit's illumination.

The man begins to run for the Wicket Gate (the fullness of the grace of Christ). His wife and children cry out to him to return, but the man runs on, crying, "Life, life, eternal life." Bunyan is not advocating desertion of one's family in a material sense. We must remember that this is a spiritual journey, not a physical one. Many go on this journey but remain bodily at home, married to their spouses, caring for their families and praying for them daily. Beginning this spiritual journey requires putting Christ foremost, as Christ advocates in Luke 14:26: "If anyone comes to Me, and does not hate his own father and mother and wife and children and brothers and sisters, yes, and even his own life, he cannot be My disciple."

We now observe how Obstinate and Pliable resolve to bring Christian back. These three characters (Christian, Obstinate, and Pliable) represent most hearers of the gospel. Matthew 13:3–8 describes them well.

> Behold, the sower went out to sow; and as he sowed, some seeds fell beside the road, and the birds came and ate them up [Obstinate]. And others fell upon the rocky places, where they did not have much soil; and immediately they sprang up, because they had no depth of soil. But when the sun had risen, they were scorched; and because they had no root, they

withered away [Pliable]. . . . And others fell on the good soil, and yielded a crop, some a hundredfold, some sixty, and some thirty [Christian]. (NASB)

Friends and comfort are more important to Obstinate than leaving the City of Destruction. Before we judge Obstinate too harshly, should we not ask ourselves what friends and/or comforts we often put before our relationship with Christ? Do we often enjoy the comfort of a warm bed rather than having a quiet time? Do we shorten our time with God so that we can spend more time with family or friends? Let us make a careful assessment of ourselves before we point our finger at others.

We see Pliable exhibiting the characteristics of his name by showing how easily he is persuaded to be of the same opinion as whomever he is with. He does this first by going along with Obstinate in trying to turn Christian back and then by going along with Christian because of Christian's glowing description of heaven. He was easily induced to engage in things of which he understood neither the nature nor the consequences. Pliable traveled with Christian because he had a desire to escape hell and obtain heaven. His struggle was for relief (earthly and spiritual) and comfort, rather than to embrace Christ in love and a seeking after holiness. Pliable did not understand that he was a sinner deserving of God's judgment for his sin as seen by the lack of a burden (conviction of sin) on his back. He had no knowledge of the sinfulness of his own heart and nature and therefore had no feeling of a need for the Savior and no desire for Christ. Pliable's low esteem of Christ is clearly seen in that the first hard time that befalls him in the slough causes him to turn back.

What is this Slough of Despond, in which Christian becomes stranded? The meaning of the Slough of Despond is described well by Bunyan in his autobiography, *Grace Abounding to the Chief of Sinners*:

My original and inward pollution, that, that was my plague and my affliction; that, I say, at a dreadful rate was always putting itself forth within me; that I had the guilt of to amazement; by reason of that I was more loathsome in my own eyes than a toad; and I thought I was so in God's eyes also. Sin and corruption would bubble up out of my heart as naturally as water bubbles up out of a fountain. I thought now that every one had a better heart than I had. I could have changed hearts with anybody. I thought none but the devil himself could equalize me for inward wickedness and pollution of mind. I fell, therefore, at the sight of my own vileness, deeply into despair, for I concluded that this condition in which I was in could not stand with a life of grace. Sure, thought I, I am forsaken of God; sure I am given up to the devil, and to a reprobate mind. (P. 31)

Distress of conscience when a true assessment of ourselves is made causes us to become discouraged in such a manner as Bunyan has described. If we do not have a good grasp of the gospel (Christ's passive and active obedience) to enable us to obtain our right standing with God, then we will fall into the slough and become despondent. We must constantly use the "steps" (the great and precious promises of God, contained in the Bible) to keep ourselves from this miry fate. Though it was not the pleasure of the King that the slough remained and he had taken measures to fix it with cartloads of wholesome instructions, the slough remained because of man's unbelief and ignorance of the Bible.

The reception given to Pliable by his neighbors upon his return home—first, they called him a wise man for coming back, then they called him a fool for going with Christian, then they mocked his cowardliness, and finally they derided Christian—illustrates the fickle and depraved nature of lost humanity.

As Christian is crossing over the field, he is deceived by self-seeking and self-satisfied Mr. Worldly Wiseman. Mr. Worldly Wiseman is in earnest for worldly prosperity, praise, and position. He makes his religion fit into his agenda. Mr. Worldly Wiseman is against any kind of religion that would interfere with a man's getting ahead in this world, trouble his mind over sin, and ruin his pleasure in satisfying his fleshly appetites. He is for using religion for secular advantage. He is a member of the "right church"—the one of which all the well-educated, wealthy, prominent people in the community are members. It does not matter what kind of theology is taught at the church; it only matters that the right kind of people attend there and that he is seen with them. The belief system Mr. Worldly Wiseman represents is that of the humanist (human wisdom). Man's way of righteousness and salvation (how to get rid of the burden) is through doing good works and living a moral life. However, because people have such a bent towards sin, they must make and observe a standard of morals at a level they are able to attain, thus lowering God's perfect standard of righteousness. They call certain sins "mistakes," not sin. And if they should actually sin, it is never their fault and, therefore, they are not accountable. They are victims of abusive parents, they were raised in poverty, they were not given the advantages of higher education, etc.

Thomas Scott has these reflections on Mr. Worldly Wiseman's arguments with Christian:

> He does not say, that Evangelist had not pointed out the way of salvation, or that wicked men are not in danger of future misery; but he urges, that so much concern about sin and the eternal world takes men off from a proper regard to their secular interests, to the injury of their families; that it prevents their enjoying comfort in domestic life, or in other providential blessings; that it leads them into perilous and distressing situation, of which their first terrors and despondings are only an earnest; that a troubled conscience may be quieted in a more expeditious and easy manner; and that they may obtain credit, comfort and manifold advantages, by following prudent counsel. (*The Pilgrim's Progress by John Bunyan*, p. 84)

Such excellent rationalizing was enough to cause poor Christian to travel a wrong path to obtain peace of conscience.

Before we leave Mr. Worldly Wiseman, Alexander Whyte would have us examine our own hearts, keeping in mind these words of advice.

> Watch yourselves well, for you all have a large piece of this worldly-wise man in yourselves. . . . It is a sure sign to you that you do not yet know the plague of your own heart, unless you know yourself to be a man more set upon the position and the praise that this world gives than you yet are on the position and the praise that come from God only. Set a watch on your own worldly heart. Watch and pray, lest you also enter into all Worldly-wiseman's temptation. (*First Series Bunyan Characters*, pp. 60–61)

Though humanists may be able to substitute their own scant obedience to the law and obtain a false peace, this is not so for Christian. As he considers his attempts to fulfill God's perfect, holy Law, he is afraid that Mount Sinai will fall on his head. We should be thankful to God for the hopeless, crushing effect of the Law, for it rescues us from works salvation, which our sinful, proud nature is so prone to pursue. Bunyan here is pointing out the danger of turning from faith in Christ to trusting in any degree in our own works for justification. Not only at death but throughout the Christian life we must approach God on Christ's merit and not in any part on our own merit. We are so tempted to think, "If I have a quiet time, if I pray daily, if I witness, this will cause God to love me more." Rather, while all these are means of grace that we may make use of to advance our sanctification, our relationship with and acceptance by God are based wholly on Christ's substitutionary atonement and his perfect obedience to the Law on behalf of his redeemed children. Christ is our righteousness (2 Corinthians 5:21) in that he has paid the penalty for our sin (on Christ's passive obedience, see Isaiah 53:6; Romans 4:25; 1 Peter 2:24; 3:18; 1 John 2:2) and has perfectly obeyed the Law for us (on Christ's active obedience, see Matthew 3:15; 5:17, 18; John 15:10; Galatians 4:4, 5; Hebrews 10:7–9).

L•E•S•S•O•N

2

Christian Rediscovers Grace

Barbour and Company, Inc. 1985, pp. 20–35
Discovery House *New Pilgrim's Progress* with notes, pp. 32–49
Moody *Pilgrim's Progress in Today's English*, pp. 27–38
Moody Classic Edition, pp. 26–40
Revell Spire Book, pp. 17–29
Whitaker House 1981 Edition, pp. 25–40

Questions for Discussion or Reflection

In this section of our story Christian arrives at the Wicket Gate, converses with Mr. Goodwill, and then enters. Continuing on his journey, he arrives at the Interpreter's house, where he is entertained for a while and is instructed in doctrinal truths as he is ushered into several rooms. Christian learns many lessons that are "rare and profitable" to his soul. May God grant that the Holy Spirit will also enlighten our understanding as we visit the Interpreter's house.

1. Christian makes haste to get back onto the Way. Arriving at he Wicket Gate, he knocks "more than once or twice." What is the meaning behind the knocking?

2. Mr. Goodwill, the Gatekeeper, asks Christian three questions. How does Christian answer these questions, and what are the important implications of his answers?

3. As Christian is about to step through the Wicket Gate, Goodwill pulls him in and warns of arrows shot from a strong castle where Beelzebub is the captain. Whom does Beelzebub represent and what do you think the arrows that are shot represent?

4. In discussing Pliable with Goodwill, Christian makes the comment, "It will appear there is no betterment betwixt him and myself." What does this statement show about the condition of Christian's heart?

5. Goodwill directs Christian to the narrow Way. How is Christian to distinguish this narrow Way?

6. Some commentators say that Mr. Interpreter represents the Holy Spirit in his teaching and enlightening capacity as we pray and as we read, hear, and meditate on Scripture. However, others say that he is a minister of the gospel and that the rooms represent various theological truths conveyed in his sermons. Mr. Interpreter had Christian come into a private room where he saw a picture. Describe the picture and tell what he learned from it that enabled him to distinguish between a false and a true minister of the gospel?

7. Mr. Interpreter takes Christian to a large parlor. What is represented by the parlor?

By the dust?

By the first sweeper?

By the second sweeper, who swept with water?

By the man choking?

8. The two rooms teach two lessons. What is taught by the private room with the picture of a grave person hanging on the wall?

By the large parlor full of dust?

9. The Interpreter next shows Christian a little room with two little children. Who are they, and whom do they represent? What lessons do they teach us? (Psalm 73 is a good commentary on this portion of the story.)

10. After this the Interpreter takes Christian to a place where a fire is burning against a wall. What does the Interpreter say is meant by the fire?

By the one who casts water on the fire?

By the oil?

By the man hidden behind the wall (2 Corinthians 12:9)?

11. What doctrinal truth about the Christian's life does the man hidden behind the wall represent?

12. The Interpreter leads Christian "into a pleasant place, where was builded a stately palace." What does the palace represent?

13. After illustrating several times in this book that heaven is not gained by good works, what then is the meaning behind the "man of stout countenance" (compare Matthew 11:12), and what are some indications that his was not a works salvation (Ephesians 6:17)?

14. Now Christian enters a very dark room where there sits a man in an iron cage. When he asks the man in the cage, "Who are you and how did you come to be in such a condition?" how does the man answer?

15. The man was lacking repentance, which God had denied him. What is repentance?

What do the following verses say concerning repentance as a gift from God alone: Romans 2:4; 2 Timothy 2:25; Acts 11:18, 5:31?

16. The man in the chamber rising out of bed was shaking and trembling. Of whom was he afraid and why?

17. "Every room in that great house was furnished and fitted up for the entertainment and instruction of pilgrims. . . . The significant rooms of that divine house instruct us also that all the lessons requisite for our salvation are not to be found in any one scripture or in any one sermon, but that all that is required by any pilgrim or any company of pilgrims should all be found in every minister's ministry as he leads his flock on from one Sabbath-day to another, rightly di-

viding the word of truth" (Whyte, *First Series Bunyan Characters*, pp.78, 80–81). Which room in the Interpreter's house was particularly profitable to your soul?

Summary and Applications

Evangelist's rebuke of Christian for becoming involved in a legalistic spirit caused Christian to make haste towards the Wicket Gate. Knocking more than once or twice at the gate indicates Christian's earnest and persistent praying and pleading with Christ in faith for mercy and forgiveness. Mr. Goodwill, the gatekeeper, comes to the gate. He is a grave man, for he continually looks at the City of Destruction, perishing men, and weary pilgrims. We are instructed in the condition of a soul seeking Christ by the answers given in response to the gatekeeper's questions. Christian realizes his sinful condition, that the world and its ways will perish, that God is holy and just, and that there is a judgment coming at which each person will stand and at which the wicked will be punished.

The arrows shot from Beelzebub's castle are those of Satan, which he lets fly with excellent aim to hit their target (the heart of man); these are arrows with which he would keep us from Christ. It is sad to think of how many people have fallen victim to these arrows. They come in the form of thoughts such as "There's plenty of time before I die; I'll come to Christ later" and "I'm too bad to come to Christ; I must reform and clean up my act first" or of satisfaction with a form of godliness, as in the case of Mr. Worldy Wiseman. Each Christian must praise the arm of Christ's omnipotent grace for pulling him or her (John 6:44) in through the gate before one of those arrows found its mark.

In Christian's statement about Pliable, "It will appear there is no betterment 'twixt him and myself," we are given a glimpse of how real grace in the heart destroys pride, humbles, and gives all glory to God for the difference there is between a Christian and a sinner.

Goodwill directs Christian to the narrow Way that has been clearly set forth by the teachings of the patriarchs, the prophets, Christ, and his apostles, which are contained in the Bible. There is objective truth to faith based on the Bible. Our faith is not to be founded on fuzzy feelings and notions, nor is it to be a blind leap of faith. Let us read our Bibles therefore with great diligence as souls lost in the wilderness who find a map directing the way back to civilization and safety.

Alexander Whyte has these thoughts on the narrow Way which Christian now sets out upon:

> There are many wide ways to hell, and many there be who crowd them, but there is only one way to heaven, and you will sometimes think you must have gone off it, there are so few companions; sometimes there will be only one footprint, with here and there a stream of blood, and always as you proceed, it becomes more and more narrow, till it strips a man bare, and sometimes threatens to close upon him and crush him to the earth altogether. Our Lord in as many words tells us all that. Strive, He says, strive every day. For many shall seek to enter into the way of salvation, but because they do not early enough, and long enough, and painfully enough strive, they come short, and are shut out. Have you, then, anything in your religious life that Christ will at last accept as the striving He intended and demanded? Does your religion cause you any real effort—Christ calls it agony? Have you ever had, do you ever have, anything that He would so describe? What cross do you every day take up? In what thing do you every day deny yourself? Name it. Put your finger on it. Write it in cipher on the margin of your Bible. Would the most liberal judgment be able to say of you that you have any fear and trembling in the work of your salvation? If not, I am afraid there must be some mistake somewhere. Christ has made it plain to a proverb, and John Bunyan has made it a nursery and schoolboy story, that the way to heaven is steep and narrow and lonely and perilous. (*First Series*, p. 70)

Christian arrives at the house of the Interpreter. I believe Bunyan meant the character of the Interpreter to represent the Holy Spirit with his enlightening and sanctifying influences on the hearts of believers. The Holy Spirit lights the candle of the Lord within our hearts, illuminating the truth. He instructs our understanding so that the Scriptures become nourishing food for our souls to feast upon. He woos us unto Christ by showing us Christ in all his loveliness and fastens our affection upon him, removing it from the temporal things of this world. From the first moment of each pilgrim's journey the

Holy Spirit gently guides, instructs, comforts, and disciplines the new joint-heir of the eternal kingdom.

Interpreter first takes Christian to a room where there is a picture of a grave man upon the wall. This picture, which represents a faithful minister of the gospel, is shown to Christian so that he might be able to distinguish a true guide (minister) from a false one. It is sobering to contemplate how many have been led astray by false guides. How we should magnify the grace of God that we too have not been led astray, and when we are led astray, how great our gratitude should be for the condescending arm of God, which graciously pulls us back!

The next room Christian visits is a large parlor. Here is "displayed the inward corruptions of the soul, and the different effects, first of the Law and afterwards of the Gospel upon them. . . . [Christian] had known most thoroughly what the Law could do with a burdened conscience; he had but begun to know what grace could do to ease it" (Cheever, *Lectures on the Pilgrim's Progress*, pp. 252–53). The Law shows us our sin but does not give us the power to subdue it. In fact the Law only "doth revive, put strength into, and increase it [sin] in the soul." As the Law reveals our holy Creator and his perfect standard (with its inward and outward demands for conformity), we are filled with anguish and terror at who we are and the condemnation we deserve. Charles Spurgeon has made this comment on the human heart, "There is nothing one half so worthy of abhorrence as the human heart. God spares from all eyes, but his own, that awful sight, a human heart; and could you and I but once see our heart, we should be driven mad, so horrible would be the sight" (*The New Park Street Pulpit*, 1:44). Only the gospel, which the Damsel and the water signify, is able to sweep and subdue the heart so that King Jesus can begin his reign in it.

The next room visited is inhabited by two little children who are completely opposite each other in character. Passion stands for the carnal men of this world, who must have everything now. Passion is discontent, for the things of this world will never satisfy creatures designed by the infinite God for a relationship with Him and for eternal things. Passion's carnal desires go against his reason and against religion. Passion misspends, by his evil lusts, what is given to him, and his conscience, heart, and character are left in rags. Patience stands for those who quietly wait for that full satisfaction that is to come, as they fix their attention on eternal realities. Patience understands that perfection and total satisfaction will never be found in this life and therefore does not expect from people, achievements, or possessions more than they are able to give. Patience strives for the things unseen (faith, humility, self-control, etc.), and Passion scorns him for this. But Patience will cheerfully part with any temporal good when it interferes with his eternal reward. It would be beneficial for us to read Psalm 73 in light of the instructions we have been given by Passion and Patience. Often we are tempted to envy the prosperity of the wicked in this world. We may lose sight of eternal realities and complain when we do not take into account the end of the wicked—in but a brief season all will be gone and their doom will be upon them. With gratitude and thanksgiving we may say with Patience, "Thou shalt guide me with thy counsel, and afterward receive me to glory. Whom have I in heaven but thee? and there is none upon earth that I desire besides thee. My flesh and my heart faileth: but God is the strength of my heart, and my portion for ever" (vv. 24–26, KJV).

The Interpreter next takes Christian by the hand and leads him into a place where a fire is burning against a wall. Here we are instructed in the doctrine of the final perseverance of the saints. Satan continually attempts to put out this flame (the work of grace) by his wicked devices. However, Christ will maintain and carry on the sanctifying work that he has begun in the soul of the believer. His standing behind the wall shows us that it is hard for us to see how this work of grace is maintained in our souls but that he is secretly feeding it and that we may rely on his secret but divine grace to carry on the sanctifying work in our souls (Philippians 1:6).

The Interpreter leads Christian to a pleasant place where there was a stately palace representing a glimpse of heaven. However, men in armor guard the palace and are resolved to harm all who try to enter. It is an empirically and biblically proven fact of life that we must enter the kingdom of God through much tribulation (Acts 14:22); and none are able to fight the battle against the enemy within (the flesh) and the enemies without (the world and the Devil) unless they have been suited with the armor of God (Ephesians 6:17). Thus, the man of stout countenance draws the sword of the Spirit, which is the Word of God, puts on the helmet of salvation, and goes forth with holy violence, determined to gain entrance no matter what the cost. Although salvation is a gift granted us by the application of Christ's work on the cross, it is a proof that God has begun this work of salvation in us if we have a violent love for Christ and a holy zeal for God's honor and glory.

Should we pause and ask ourselves how violent we are in our pursuit of God's kingdom? Where are the zeal and holy violence today that were displayed by Paul, by George Whitefield, by Jonathan Edwards? A famous pastor once said, "Give me six thorough red-hot Christians and I will do more, by God's grace, with them, than six hundred ordinary |lukewarm| professors. I would as soon hunt with dead dogs as try to work with them." How hot are we on the thermometer of zeal when it comes to our prayers, witnessing, mortifying the flesh, reading the Scriptures, and attending to the Word preached? A lazy, careless attitude toward Christ and his kingdom is not how the Bible describes the Christian life, for Matthew 11:12 says, "The kingdom of heaven suffers violence, and violent men take it by force." This picture of mingled encouragement and warning is meant to prepare us for the many conflicts that are a part of the Christian pilgrimage.

J. C. Ryle gives us a vivid description of the battlefield in these comments:

> The Christian's fight is a good fight, because fought with the best of issues and results. No doubt it is a war in which there are tremendous struggles, agonizing conflicts, wounds, bruises, watchings, fastings, and fatigue. But still every believer, without exception, is "more than conqueror through Him that loved him." No soldiers of Christ are ever lost, missing, or left dead on the battlefield. No mourning will ever need to be put on, and no tears to be shed for either private or officer in the army of Christ. The muster roll, when the last evening comes, will be found precisely the same that it was in the morning. The English guards marched out of London to the Crimean campaign a magnificent body of men; but many of the gallant fellows laid their bones in a foreign grave, and never saw London again. Far different shall be the arrival of the Christian army in "the city which hath foundations, whose builder and maker is God." Not one shall be found lacking. The words of our great Captain shall be found true: "Of them which Thou hast given Me I have lost none" (John 18:9). (*Holiness*, p. 62)

Though the battles we fight in this life are numerous, long, and hard, sweet shall be the victory and great the reward when Christ, our great Captain, shall turn to us and say, "Well done, thou good and faithful servant" (Matthew 25:21).

A solemn warning awaits Christian in the dark room to which he is next taken. A man in a cage laments his present situation. He tells Christian that he was once a "fair and flourishing professor," but through unfaithfulness (the lusts, pleasures, and profits of this world), sin and despair had seized him. The man had a knowledge of his sin, but there is no indication that God had given him true repentance. True repentance consists not only in recognizing sin and its danger but also in seeing its ugliness, as a result of which one grieves for and hates sin because it is offensive to the holy, gracious God of the universe, whose mercy has been exhibited through Christ's atoning sacrifice. There must be a desire to forsake sin for the right reasons if it is true evangelical repentance. As Spurgeon has stated. "Men who only believe their depravity but do not hate it are no further than the devil on the road to heaven. . . . True repentance is a turning of the *heart*, as well as the *life*; it is the giving up of the whole soul to God, to be his forever and ever; it is a renunciation of the sins of the heart as well as the crimes of life" (*New Park Street Pulpit*, 5:85). The man in the cage teaches us not to venture one step on so dangerous a path as he took in his willful sinning and to cling to Christ in prayer and obedient conduct.

The Interpreter next bids Christian tarry to see one more thing, a man rising out of bed, who "shook and trembled" at the dream he had had. What terrified the dreamer was that the Day of Judgment had come and he was not ready for it. The sinful world we live in, along with the Devil, seeks to hide the fact that there is a Day of Judgment coming, and a great many consciences are easily lulled to sleep by this deception. Only as people are exposed to the truth contained in the Bible are they awakened from this deadly soul-sleep. Oh, that we could cause more people to shake and tremble before it is too late and the Judgment Day is upon us.

Christian learns from his visit with the Interpreter that where there is a gospel hope, there will be a godly fear; both are necessary, and both are graces of the Holy Spirit.

L·E·S·S·O·N
3
The Path to House Beautiful

Barbour and Company, Inc. 1985, pp. 35–58
Discovery House *New Pilgrim's Progress* with notes, pp. 49–71
Moody *Pilgrim's Progress in Today's English*, pp. 39–55
Moody Classic Edition, pp. 40–62
Revell Spire Book, pp. 29–48
Whitaker House 1981 Edition, pp. 41–63

Questions for Discussion or Reflection

In lesson 3 we will proceed to the cross, where Christian finds and feels the comfort of the faith he has believed, thus losing his burden. Next Christian comes upon Simple, Sloth, and Presumption, all fast asleep. Gaining insights from this encounter, we will continue with Christian as he has a lively conversation with Formalist and Hypocrisy and ascends the hill called Difficulty. Continuing our journey with the pilgrim, we will meet two enemies of the Christian faith, Timorous and Mistrust, who have turned and are going back. Because of his lack of diligence and his indulgence of the flesh, Christian has a temporary setback. He, however, recovers and makes haste and is welcomed at the house called Beautiful.

1. Where does Christian lose his burden, and where does it go? Can you think of some verses that confirm this truth?

2. Why do you think "springs that were in his [Christian's] head sent waters down his cheeks"?

3. Who do you think the three Shining Ones are, and what is the significance of their words and actions to Christian?

4. Christian sees three men fast asleep with fetters upon their heels. Here is shown the misery and danger of so-called professors, to warn us and cause us to be watchful and diligent. Name them and give a description of each type of person.

What do the fetters represent?

5. What were the names of the two men who came "tumbling over the wall"?

Where were they from, where were they going, and for what purpose were they going there?

What did the wall represent, and what was omitted from their pilgrimage that Christian had not omitted?

What was the reason the two men gave for their not coming in as Christian had?

What were they counted as by the Lord of the Way?

6. The hill called Difficulty represents circumstances that require self-denial and exertion. Though it is a way unpleasing to our flesh and blood, this way proves the sincerity of our faith. As Christian is going up the hill Difficulty, he stops midway at a pleasant arbor. What happens to him there?

What lesson for our own lives do we learn from this incident?

7. When Christian gets to the top of the hill, two men meet him, Timorous and Mistrust. Though they frighten Christian with their report of the danger of the Way, how does he shake off this fear?

8. What puts Christian in great distress? Why? What does he do next to remedy the situation?

9. Christian beholds a very stately palace before him, the name of which is Beautiful, so he makes haste towards it. However, two lions are in the way. What do the lions represent and why were they placed there?

10. Christian seeks entrance into the palace called Beautiful. Whom does the porter represent?

What does the palace Beautiful represent?

Whom does the grave and beautiful damsel, Discretion, represent, and what questions does she ask?

11. Christian is introduced to three more ladies. Piety (who demonstrates a sincere and earnest desire to do God's will) asks Christian, "What moved you at first to betaken yourself to a Pilgrim's Life?" How does Christian answer her? What three things which impressed him in the Interpreter's house does Christian relate to Piety?

Prudence (who demonstrates an ability to govern and discipline oneself) asks questions concerning his inward desire and temptations to indulge in the sins of the flesh. What are some of the questions she asks and how does Christian respond?

Charity (love) questions Christian about his family. What reasons did Christian's family give for not coming with him?

12. "A holy and heavenly life is a continual pain to the consciences of sinners around you and continually solicits them to change their course" (Richard Baxter). This statement is shown to be true by Christian's family. What was the response of his family to his "Conversation" (way of life)?

13. They sit together talking until supper is ready. What supper does this remind you of, at which Christians come together to feed on Jesus by faith, and contemplate what he has done for them and is now doing for them at the right hand of God?

What remarks made at the supper did you find new or interesting?

14. In the morning Christian is taken into the study. Is what happens in the study similar to any morning time that you have had? How?

15. What provisions, made in Christ, for maintaining and increasing a Christian's strength and victory over his enemies were found in the armory?

Summary and Application

Leaving the Interpreter's house, Christian runs up the highway with great difficulty because of the burden on his back. A person may be in Christ and yet have a deep sense of the burden of sin, which may remain for a time. As the Holy Spirit teaches us the truths of the glorious gospel (John 16:14), we become able to comprehend Christ and his work on the cross more fully. When Christian gets a fuller view of the cross and rests all his hopes there, then his burden tumbles off and he feels the comfort of his evangelical belief. If a Christian does not have this peace and release from the burden of sin, it is in part because of ignorance, through error or neglect, of the gospel.

Three Shining Ones come to Christian and salute him. Here is shown the love and grace of God the Father, God the Son, and God the Holy Spirit. God, the judge of the universe, declares, "Thy sins are forgiven thee" because of Christ's substitutionary atonement. Christ then strips Christian of his rags and clothes him in robes of righteousness (Isaiah 61:10). The Holy Spirit sets a mark on his forehead signifying a renewed mind, which will appear in holy living and an open profession of faith. The roll is given as a sign of assurance of acceptance; this acceptance is made apparent as the believer sees his views, desires, and purposes come to line up with Scripture.

Christian finds "three men fast asleep with fetters upon their heels." These men appear to be pilgrims "asleep a little out of the Way." They are not aware of their desperate situation and seem to think all is well. Any attempts to warn them of their danger are futile. We see this reckless attitude many times when we share the gospel, as Cheever describes it:

Simple said, I see no danger. That was the voice of one-third part of the world in their sins. Tell them they are sleeping on the brink of perdition, and they say, We see no danger. Sloth said, Yet a little more sleep. That was the voice of another third part of the world. A little longer indulgence in sin is pleaded for, a little more quiet ease and indifference; wait till we have a more convenient season; a little more folding of the hands to sleep! Presumption said, Every vat must stand on its own bottom. There outspoke at least another third part of the world in their sins. Take care of your interests, and I will take care of mine. You need not trouble yourself about my salvation. I am not at all concerned but that all will go well, and I am ready to take my chance. (*Lectures on the Pilgrim's Progress*, p. 279)

Death and judgment will awake at last these deluded men who sleep on in their false security.

Two men come tumbling over the wall, taking what they perceive to be a shortcut. Christian questions their course, as he considers the Word of God the only rule of faith and conduct. His new acquaintances, Formalist and Hypocrisy, cannot be troubled with repentance for sin, seeking after holiness (which is found only in Christ), and depending on the indwelling Holy Spirit. They are content with going through the motions of religion, without understanding it or having their affections placed on Christ. Their religion is all rites and ceremonies without substance. They seek the applause of men in all that they do in the way of religious duties. They do not like to be questioned about their real motives for what they do, and they shun the fact that their sin will damn them unless they are found in Christ. Their faith is all outward actions, not inward truth. Spurgeon shows us the difference between a formalist and hypocrite in this description: "Hypocrisy was the bigger rogue of the two, for he had not any belief in the matter at all. Formalist had, perhaps, some measure of faith of a certain sort; he thought there might be something in form and ceremonies. But Hypocrisy said in his heart, 'Ah, it is all a pretty story, but then it is a very respectable story; and if I pretend to believe it, people will think the better of me'" (*Pictures from Pilgrim's Progress*, p. 95). We are further warned of how easy it is to pass from being a formalist to being a hypocrite in these words from Alexander Whyte:

31

A formalist is not yet a hypocrite exactly, but he is ready now and well on the way at any moment to become a hypocrite. As soon now as some temptation shall come to him to make appear another and a better man than he really is: when in some way it becomes his advantage to seem to other people to be a spiritual man: when he thinks he sees his way to some profit or praise by saying things and doing things that are not true and natural to him,—then he will pass on from being a bare and simple formalist, and will henceforth become a hypocrite. He has never had any real possession or experience of spiritual things amid all his formal observances of religious duties, and he has little or no difficulty, therefore, in adding another formality or two to his former life of unreality. And thus the transition is easily made from a comparatively innocent and unconscious formalist to a conscious and studied hypocrite. (*First Series Bunyan Characters*, p. 134)

Samuel Rutherford has said, "The worst of hypocrites is he who whitens himself till he deceives himself" (ibid., p. 136). It is most important to understand that it is not in human nature to deceive others for any long period of time without in a measure deceiving ourselves also.

Bunyan next shows us how the formalist and the hypocrite show their true colors when the group comes to the hill called Difficulty. We learn the peril of turning out of the Way and the fate of those who do so as we read the names of these supposedly easier paths, Danger and Destruction. It is hard to counterfeit spiritual graces, such as love for Christ, sincere striving for the glory and honor of God, etc. Many are the forms of the hill called Difficulty in the Christian life in which true grace is exhibited. Often we think of physical difficulties that come our way, but just as difficult are acts of self-denial, the experiences of humbling our proud hearts, not seeking the praise of men, overcoming sinful habits of the flesh, and graciously forgiving ingratitude and injury done to us. With both physical and spiritual difficulties our faith is proved to be genuine and made to grow, so up the hill Difficulty the Christian must go. A Christian's climb up the hill Difficulty is not easy; it is usually a slow, long, arduous ascent. God may give us a season of refreshment in which we may rest, but this is not meant to be a place where we tarry too long. Often we become self-satisfied with where we are in our Christian walk and do not go forward. We forget that we must grow in the grace and knowledge of the Lord Jesus Christ and that we must press forward towards the mark for the prize of the high call of God in Christ. This is what happens to Christian at the arbor. He becomes so well satisfied with himself, his roll, his robe, and his acceptance with God that he sleeps in an arbor not designed for sleep but for rest and refreshment.

Christian is mercifully awakened with a warning and runs up to the top of the hill. In his haste and because of his carelessness he leaves his roll (assurance). This leaves him vulnerable to distress and anguish when the first trial comes his way. A great deal of sorrow could have been avoided if Christian had not let himself indulge in sleep. Watchfulness is at all times necessary on this side of heaven, for our enemies are ever awake and seeking to do us harm. It seems that many times we are wide awake when it comes to temporal interests but sleepy and slothful when it comes to the much more important matter of our eternal souls. Eternity will reveal how much spiritual profit our souls have missed by our sleepiness; how many quiet times were slept through, Sunday services were drowsily attended, prayer times were missed, and opportunities for witnessing or discipleship were lost, and how much preparedness for Bible studies forfeited because of our spiritual slumber. We see the sad result of this sleepiness (lack of communion with God) in the loss of power, zeal, and joy in the lives of so many Christians. May God grant us the realization of what we have lost and enable us to mend our pace.

As Christian reaches the top of the hill, he meets Timorous and Mistrust running full of terror the other way. They have just conquered the hill and then had seen two lions in the path. Thus their assessment of the pilgrimage (the Christian life) is that the farther you go, the more danger and trouble there is. However, there is no turning back for Christian, for he knows that he will certainly perish if he does so. Feeling for his roll to gain comfort, he discovers that it is missing. Realizing that his indulgence of the flesh by sleeping in the arbor has caused him to lose his roll, he asks God for forgiveness and hurries back to search for it. Christians suffer temporary setbacks when they are not alert and aggressive in the Christian life, and these cause them to lose their assurance and joy and many other blessings that sustain them in the trials they must face. Commenting on this ease of the flesh, Cheever states: "This is what Christians are often doing, and this evil is certainly a great one, of using for indulgence and ease to the flesh what God has given us to minister to the advancement of our spirits. We are not anxious enough to be making progress towards heaven; we are too fond of comfort, and too averse from labor" (Lectures, p. 292). O God, enable us to use the seasons of grace that you grant us for the building up of our spiritual muscles for those times of struggle that are so often upon us.

By God's gracious dealing with Christian, he finds his roll and hurries towards the palace named Beautiful (the church). He sees the two lions that had been reported to him by Timorous and Mistrust. These lions represent hindrances to joining the church. On this present challenge Spurgeon remarks:

> Unbelief generally has a good eye for the lions, but a blind eye for the chains that hold them back. It is quite true that there are difficulties in the way of those who profess to be followers of the Lord Jesus Christ. We do not desire to conceal this fact, and we do not wish you to come amongst us without counting the cost. But it is also true that these difficulties have a limit which they cannot pass. Like the lions in the pilgrim's pathway, they are chained, and restrained, and absolutely under the control of the Lord God Almighty. (Pictures, p. 115)

The lions frighten Christian so much that he considers turning back, but the porter, whose name is Watchful, encourages him to come, for the lions are chained. A minister of Christ, which the porter represents, must be watchful for the good of souls, giving encouragement and advice to pilgrims.

By placing the house Beautiful early in Christian's journey, Bunyan shows the importance he places on a Christian's uniting with a local body of believers. When a person becomes a Christian, he or she becomes a member of Christ's body, the invisible church. Many do not hold membership in the visible church in high regard because of this concept (of believers' already being a part of the invisible church). However, every member of the invisible church should be a member of a visible church congregation, for it is Christ himself who desires this and joins believers to the visible church (Acts 2:47). While Scripture teaches that membership in a church is not a prerequisite of salvation, it is a usual consequence thereof. It is also the God-assigned task of the church to dispense the means of grace—the Word and the sacraments. . . . By the preaching of the Word and the administration of the sacraments the church nurtures her members and builds them up in faith. To be sure, for results the church is utterly dependent on the grace of the Holy Spirit. Only when God blesses the means of grace will they prove effective. But the fact remains that God has committed to the church the means for spiritual growth. (Kuiper, *The Glorious Body of Christ*, pp. 112–13)

Another important reason for uniting with the visible church is the submission of oneself to the discipline of the church (Matthew 18:15–18; Galatians 6:1–2). For those who have placed themselves under the authority of the leadership of a local church, we see why it is important that they be members of a church with whose statement of faith, leadership, and preaching they agree (from their study of Scripture). Sadly, today there is not a proper view and understanding of the visible church, and this has contributed to her weakness.

Though Christian desires to enter, he is not immediately admitted to the palace Beautiful without some inquiry into his profession of faith. It is very proper to seek external evidences of a person's faith, but of course only God can see the internal evidence, the heart in which he has worked an act of grace (regeneration). The porter calls four virgins to speak with Christian.

Discretion is the first to question Christian. Discretion represents the elders and/or deacons of a church by whom prospective members are examined. Her first question, "Whence he came," is asked to ascertain if he knew what he was by nature; for if you do not know that you are a sinner (by birth and actions), you do not really begin to know anything aright. She also asks him how he got into the Way, which was another important question. Christian had already had several characters introduce to him their own "ways" of entering and Discretion is pleased to hear that he has come the correct way through the Wicket Gate. The admission of members into churches should be done with discretion, for none should be admitted into the church but those who can give others good reasons to believe that they are indeed sincere pilgrims on the way to the Celestial City.

The next damsel to speak with Christian is Piety. The personification of this part of the church is important, for without true piety (a sincere desire to do God's will) there can be no real Christianity and only a weak and ineffective church. Piety has Christian review his journey thus far so that God's glory, power, and grace in his keeping of Christian may be demonstrated. This is also a way of increasing Christian's humility, gratitude, and faith.

In the conversation with Prudence, Christian is made to examine his heart. Prudence represents believers who understand spiritual matters and know how to search the heart. Prudence inquires into the struggle Christian has in his soul and the conflict that still goes on between his sin nature and grace. We are here reminded of Romans 7 and Paul's battle involving the good that he desires to do and the evil that he does. Prudence asks Christian how he vanquishes this enemy of his soul. His response is indeed suitable, for it is by the cross that we are enabled to conquer sin, remembering him who hung upon that cross. With this gazing upon Christ comes a desire to be with him in glory and to gain the sweet victory that there will be over the sin we have struggled with in this life.

Charity, who judges kindly, yet justly, according to the love of Christ that is shed abroad in her heart, now asks Christian about his family. He shares with Charity his earnest striving and praying for his wife and four sons to flee from the danger he perceived and come to Christ. Christian realized that the life of a believer carries as much conviction and persuasion as his words, and therefore he sought to avoid giving "occasion by any unseemly action to make them averse to going on the pilgrimage." A believer who allows his life to be full of sin will harden others against the things of God; therefore, we should study and pray to live a life of holiness. We should also examine our lives to see if we have done harm to Christ's cause by our unholy walk.

The supper at which they sit down is the Lord's Supper. Here believers are invited to feed on Jesus by faith and are nourished by him unto eternal life. It is a time to dwell in contemplation, wonder, love, and praise for what Jesus has done for us as we consider the cross (his atonement for our sin); his dwelling in us (by the Holy Spirit), enabling us to live holy lives; his intercession for us at the right hand of God; and his blessed return for his church.

> The Lord's supper is more than a memorial, it is a fellow-ship, a communion. Those who eat of this bread, spiritually understanding what they do, those who drink of this cup, en-

tering into the real meaning of that reception of the wine, do therein receive Christ spiritually into their hearts. Their heart, soul, mind feeds upon Christ himself, and upon what Christ has done. We do not merely record that fact, but we enjoy the result of it. We do not merely say that Christ died; but we desire to die with him, and to live only as the result of his having died. We take scot and lot with Christ as we come to the table. (Spurgeon, *The Metropolitan Tabernacle*, 39:218)

After having his soul melted by the love of Christ exhibited at the table, Christian lies down in a large upper chamber the name of which is Peace. Peace of conscience and serenity of mind are the results of a true profession of faith, communion with Christ, and fellowship with other believers.

In the morning a delightful time is had in the study as they go over "records of the greatest antiquity." This reading about and meditating upon the wondrous works of God should be the way each Christian enjoys starting his or her day. Here are found sweet experiences of God and invigoration for the soul.

Christian leaves the house called Beautiful after being given a glimpse of the Delectable Mountains, which are a foretaste of heaven, and being suited up in the armory. He has been refreshed and edified by the sights he has seen and instruction he has received there. However, there was a mutual edification, as expressed by Cheever's comments: "He was instructed with much godly conversation, and with many edifying sights, and he was clad in a complete suit of armor, to prepare him against the dangers of the future way. On his part, he entertained the household as much as they did him, by the account he gave of his own experience thus far" (*Lectures*, p. 300).

L·E·S·S·O·N
4
Lessons from the Valleys of Humiliation and Death

Barbour and Company, Inc. 1985, pp. 58–71
Discovery House *New Pilgrim's Progress* with notes, pp. 73–84
Moody *Pilgrim's Progress in Today's English*, pp. 56–65
Moody Classic Edition, pp. 62–74
Revell Spire Book, pp. 48–58
Whitaker House 1981 Edition, pp. 64–76

Questions for Discussion or Reflection

In our last lesson we saw how Christian was edified and encouraged at the house called Beautiful. In this portion of the story Christian walks through two valleys. In the first valley he has a terrible battle with a foul fiend. New trials meet Christian as he passes through the next valley. However, not even these adversities are able to stop his progress. We have some exciting spiritual truths to learn in this lesson. Let us make haste and press forward.

1. After being favored with many spiritual blessings at the house called Beautiful, Christian departs. Where does he go next, and why do you think this place was chosen by Bunyan to be next in the pilgrim's journey?

2. A foul fiend meets Christian. What is his name? (See Revelation 9:11.)

He perceives that Christian had been one of his subjects. What were the wages he paid him? (See Romans 6:23.)

3. What did Christian like better about "the prince under whose banner" he now stood?

4. What were some of the subtle reasonings this foul fiend used to dissuade Christian from persevering in the way he was going and to switch his allegiance from the King of princes he was now under?

What were some of Christian's responses to him?

5. Why was the battle between Christian and his foe so severe?

6. Christian now enters the Valley of the Shadow of Death. On the basis of the description that is given of it, what do you think is the meaning of this valley?

7. On the right hand of the valley there is a ditch and on the left hand a quag. What do you think the ditch represents?

What do you think the quag represents? Who fell into the quag, and who plucked him out?

8. What weapon did Christian find useful in the midst of the valley?

Why do you believe this was the best weapon at this point in his journey?

9. "When Christian had traveled in this disconsolate condition some considerable time, he thought he heard the voice of a man, as going before him, saying, Though I walk through the Valley of the Shadow of Death, I will fear none Ill, for thou art with me." What were the three reasons why Christian was glad?

Summary and Applications

The four damsels from the house called Beautiful accompany the pilgrim to the Valley of Humiliation. There is an ever-present danger for Christians who have been well fed and favored with special blessings to become puffed up; therefore, for the good of the soul, the flesh must be humbled and kept low lest spiritual pride exist. It is hard to go down into the Valley of Humiliation without slipping into murmuring and discontent and questioning God as to why events are happening. Believers must continually remind themselves that it is God who knows what is best, not they, and must desire what will bring God the most glory.

In this valley Christian meets Apollyon (signifying the destroyer, Revelation 9:11), and here he tries out his armor. Bunyan has not illustrated the Christian life on earth as a vacation in paradise spent sitting on the beach in a lawn chair. Christian has been given weapons to fight with, not play with. It is the mind-set of our present day that this life is to be full of ease and comfort. The abundant life Christ spoke of is understood to mean physical comforts of every kind. The teachings of Christ and the apostles were quite different. Their preaching was about athletes in training, strangers and aliens to this world, and great battles to be fought and won. The battle that is raging for the souls of men demands that we be suited at all times with the complete armor of God, and any soldier who would put down his sword or misplace any of his armor during battle is to be considered most foolish.

Satan hurls darts that tempt us to pride, carelessness, presumption, self-confidence, mistrust of God, and despair. He tells us that by going down so low in this valley we are going out of the way of influence and usefulness. He tells us that great things cannot be done for God when we are so low. And he tells us that such a great light as ours should not be hidden but put in a prominent place for the good of all. In this and many other ways, Satan uses subtle and artful reasonings to prevent pilgrims from persevering in the ways of the Lord.

Though tempted to flee and run, Christian realizes that he has no armor for his back and so there is no safety except in facing his enemy. The fierce battle that ensues would cause the stoutest Christian to give way, except for the fact that in every conflict with Satan the battle is the Lord's. It is his strength that is engaged for our victory.

Apollyon's accusations against Christian rightly earn him the title "accuser of the brethren" (Revelation 12:10), but Christian counters him by exaggerating his charges and thus exalting the grace and mercy of God in pardoning so freely. Also, Christian claims that he now groans under and sorrows over the remaining evils. We then see how such humbling of ourselves and exalting of Christ puts Satan in a rage. Apollyon tells Christian to prepare to die. Christian uses the shield of faith (the belief that he has been justified by Christ's work on the cross and is being sanctified daily) to deflect Apollyon's flaming darts. The Lord appears to have forsaken Christian as he falls on his back and loses his sword. Just when Christian is ready "to despair of life," he is helped by the special grace of God to seize his sword. In a believer's greatest battles the Holy Spirit will bring to mind the precious promises found in the Scriptures and enable the believers to rely on them.

As Apollyon flees, Christian looks upward and smiles. This was not a proud, boastful smile at what he had accomplished but a humble, thankful smile giving God all the glory for the victory won that day.

The battle of Christian with Apollyon lasted more than half a day, but the battle of Christian with himself and the various allurements of the world lasted all the way from the Wicket Gate to the River Jordan. We will see the various allurements of the world and how Christian copes with them when we visit Vanity Fair. As for the battle with himself, we have caught a partial view of it while going through the Valley of Humiliation with him. This battle, the plague of his own heart, will be detected more fully as various circumstances arise. May we use these views as a mirror for our own lives.

We have just been through the Valley of Humiliation, where we have seen how God humbles believers by adverse circumstances, whether they be bodily illnesses, financial setbacks, times of being passed over rather than advanced in a job, etc. There we saw how Satan takes advantage of us and attacks us when we are down. We are now introduced to another valley. This Valley of the Shadow of Death illustrates the times of spiritual distress that we all go through—such times as when our worship seems hollow and dull, whereas once it was lively and full of joy; when God seems to hide his countenance and divine things appear obscure and almost unreal; when our religious duties become a burden rather than a delight and we become weary in the ongoing battle with sin in our hearts and despair of ever conquering it. The valley becomes all the darker as believers are tempted to doubt that God is in control. Some have longer and darker times in this valley than others. Bunyan was very familiar with this valley, as is made apparent in his autobiography.

Though this valley of spiritual depression may not be visible to the human eye, it is nonetheless real and stressful. Cheever explains it in this way:

> We are naturally less affected with sympathy for men's spiritual distresses, than we are for their temporal or bodily evils. The reason is to be found in our want of spiritual experience, and in the fact that we habitually look at, and are moved by, the things which are seen, and not the things which are unseen. We are creatures of sense, and therefore a great battle, when a kingdom is to be lost or won, affects us more deeply than the far more sublime and awful conflict, where the soul and the kingdom of heaven are to be lost or won forever. (*Lectures on the* Pilgrim's Progress, p. 331)

So we learn that this is a lonely valley, for there are few who will sympathize with such distress of soul as a person has here.

On the border of the Shadow of Death Christian meets two men who bring an evil report of the Way. They endeavor to excuse their own apostasy by relating the many dangers they have seen from a distance but have never actually experienced. Christian does well to give them as little time as possible and to use the conversation with them to incite diligence by drawing his sword.

On the right hand of this valley is a very deep ditch representing false doctrines causing false security. Many men have been led there. On the left is a quag representing despair of God's mercy after falling into sin (such as King David experienced, Psalm 32:3, 4). In times of spiritual depression one may easily fall into one or the other of these two extremes (i.e., fearlessness because of incorrect teaching or hopelessness because of despair). The exceeding narrowness of the Way shows how careful we must be in regard to these ditches and quags.

Christian passes hard by the mouth of hell in the midst of the valley. Such were the sparks and hideous noises coming out of this hole, which cared not for Christian's sword (the Word of God), that he was forced to use another weapon, which was called All-prayer. Many are the times when a person is so distressed that he is not even able to read the Word of God but can only cry out in agonizing prayer to God and cling to Christ.

As if this valley were not dreadful and dark enough, now a fiend whispers horrid blasphemies into Christian's ear in such a manner that he thinks they are coming from his own mind. Poor Christian does not realize that his distress over such thoughts shows that their disposition is the opposite of his heart and that his dislike of them is proof of his love for God.

Christian is encouraged by the voice of another pilgrim and hopes for the communion and encouragement a fellow believer is sure to give. For the present, however, this sweet communion is not to be.

We wonder, "Why does God have Christians travel through such a dreadful valley?" Shall we not look back over the valley in daylight and realize how sweet are the uses of adversity in God's hand as they humble us, cause us to earnestly seek Him, and purge us of our sins? "Wonderful are the wisdom and mercy of God, in making the spiritual temptations and distresses of his people their necessary discipline for their highest good, the means for the greatest perfection and stability of their characters" (ibid., p. 348). What is strange, though, is that we are not able to learn by reading about the experiences of others in this valley but must be made to believe these truths from our own experience.

> Every pilgrim in turn has to go through this Valley, has to learn by himself both the dreadful evils of the heart, and the power of temptation, and the greatness of deliverance by the Almighty power and love of the Savior. He cannot learn this by hearing others tell it to him; God must teach him by the

precious costly way of personal discipline. He can no more come to the stature of a perfect man in Christ Jesus without this discipline, than a baby could grow up to manhood without learning at first to creep, then to walk, then to speak, to read, to exercise all faculties. The great discipline which we need as pilgrims is mostly the experience of our own weakness, and the art of finding our strength in Christ; but it is astonishing what severe treatment is oftentimes necessary to teach this, apparently the simplest and most obvious of all lessons, but yet the deepest and most difficult to be learned. (Ibid., pp. 349–50)

L•E•S•S•O•N
5
Christian Meets Faithful

Barbour and Company, Inc. 1985, pp. 71–95
Discovery House *New Pilgrim's Progress* with notes, pp. 84–104
Moody *Pilgrim's Progress in Today's English*, pp. 66–86
Moody Classic Edition, pp. 74–96
Revell Spire Book, pp. 58–78
Whitaker House 1981 Edition, pp. 77–101

Questions for Discussion or Reflection

Christian is now joined in his journey by Faithful, and they share in some profitable conversation. Faithful gives an account of his own time in the Valley of Humiliation. We see how different his experience in this valley was from Christian's. Truly the Christian life is not a "cookie cutter" experience with all believers' lives exactly the same. The enemies and trials along the way are varied for each of us. Finally we will meet Talkative. In Bunyan's description of this gospel hypocrite we will be able to see very clearly the difference between mere intellectual assent to doctrinal truths of the gospel and having the experience of grace and power in a regenerate heart to enable us to believe and live out these truths.

1. Leaving the valley, Christian sees Faithful before him upon the Way. What happens next, and what lesson do you learn from it?

2. As Christian talks to Faithful and shares his experiences since leaving the City of Destruction, what former companion of Christian's does Faithful say that he has heard talk about, and what had he heard?

3. Although Faithful had not fallen into the Slough, whom had he met that "had liked to have done [him] mischief"?

What are some of the means she employs to attack us today?

What had she promised him, and what could she not give?

4. Faithful came to the foot of the hill called Difficulty. Whom did he meet there?

What were the names of the three daughters? Describe some characteristics (or the nature) of each one.

What would have happened to Faithful if he had gone to this man's house?

What was the warning written on the old man's forehead, and what are the implications of this warning for us?

5. Faithful meets with a man who comes after him as swift as the wind. Who is he?

What does this man represent?

Why does he strike Faithful down?

The man would have continued beating Faithful if it had not been for whom?

6. In the Valley of Humiliation Faithful meets Discontent. What does he try to persuade Faithful to do, and what are his reasons for this advice?

What was Faithful's reply to him?

Have you ever had a conversation with Discontent? What was your reply to him?

7. Next Faithful is attacked by Shame. What are some of the objections Shame brings against religion?

There is no stronger proof of our fallen, sinful condition than the fact that we are prone to be ashamed of the things of God. Has this ever been true in your life?

What comments made by Faithful will enable you to respond correctly to Shame?

8. In Talkative's beginning conversation with Faithful, he is able to spew out orthodox doctrine he has learned but only like a parrot. What is the first indication Talkative gives that shows that his heart is unchanged?

What indications does Christian give of Talkative's true condition?

Is Christian being disobedient to Titus 3:2 when he speaks evil of Talkative? Explain your answer.

9. Having been convinced of Talkative's hypocrisy, Faithful asks the question of Christian, "What shall we do to be rid of him?" Christian suggests that Faithful "enter into some serious discourse about the power of religion." With what pointed remarks is Faithful able to carry out this suggestion?

10. How does Faithful say a work of grace in the soul is discovered?

After accusing Faithful of being "some peevish or melancholy man," Talkative bids him adieu. John Gulliver comments thus on this section: "Heart-searching, soul-examining, and close questioning of the conduct of life, will not do with talkative professors. Ring a peal on the doctrines of grace, and many will chime in with you; but speak closely how grace operates upon the heart, and influences the life to follow Christ in self-denying obedience, they cannot bear it: they are offended with you, and will turn away from you, and call you legal" (*The Complete Works of John Bunyan*, p. 130).

11. Christian commends Faithful for his plain dealing with Talkative and states, "There is but little of this faithful dealing with men now a days." What reasons does he give for the importance of reproving such Talkatives?

Summary and Applications

God graciously gives Christian a companion in fellow pilgrim Faithful. When Christian catches up to and overruns Faithful, a lesson in pride and humility is learned as Christian stumbles and falls. He who was patting himself on the back for having overrun his brother is now helped up by the very one he had so underestimated. Such are the lessons that God teaches us, that when we have an inflated ego (spiritual pride), the very one we feel superior to is usually the one who will help us in our distress.

Faithful and Christian fall into a useful conversation about Faithful's experiences since leaving the City of Destruction. With this conversation the author seeks to show how Faithful's pilgrimage had differed from Christian's, thus avoiding the error of making one pilgrimage exactly the same as another. Many are the twists and turns of each man's venture towards the Celestial City; nonetheless, the pilgrims must continually move forward, for retreat will bring certain ruin.

Faithful describes how, although he had escaped the Slough of Despond, he had met with Wanton. She pleaded hard and promised very enticing returns. We must use Joseph's way of conquering such gross sin, running from her. "Flee from youthful lusts," wrote Paul to Timothy (2 Timothy 2:22). Each of us has partial knowledge of our weakest areas concerning sin. If going to an R-rated movie will expose a weak area, we should shun any such activity. Wanton uses many things that in and of themselves are all right—until they are perverted by sin. Faithful did not yield to Wanton's tempting but he stated, "I know not whether I did wholly escape her or no." On this Spurgeon comments:

> The probability is, that the temptations of the flesh, even when resisted, do us an injury. If the coals do not burn us, they blacken us. The very thought of evil, and especially of such evil, is sin. We can hardly read a newspaper report of anything of this kind without having our minds in some degree defiled. There are certain flowers which perfume the air as they bloom, and I may say of these matters that they scatter an ill savor as they are repeated in our ears. (*Pictures from Pilgrim's Progress*, pp. 146–47)

Deliver us, Lord, from the pit into which we will certainly be cast if we yield to Wanton's flattering tongue.

Next, Faithful recounts how at the foot of the hill called Difficulty he had met Adam the first, who is a personification of our sin nature, which is ours because of Adam's original sin. Adam the first asked Faithful to go home with him and promised him wages. And what were the wages promised? A sure inheritance, for "the wages of sin is death" (Romans 6:23); and we will inherit, if we abide with him, what the old Adam left us (we are heirs of wrath). The work promised Faithful would be "many delights." Yes, for the carnal man there is pleasure in sin, but there is no contentment and there are often undesirable consequences. Old Adam has three daughters. Unfortunately, we all know them intimately. Of these gals Spurgeon gives the following description:

> The Lust of the Flesh, we have already spoken [of] under the head of wantonness. Then there is the Lust of the Eyes. The eye can scarcely look upon a thing of beauty without desiring it. We soon become covetous unless the Spirit of God keeps our mind under proper restraint. 'Thou shalt not covet,' is a commandment which is often broken by us almost unconsciously. Consequently, we do not repent as we should of our sin against that commandment which touches our thoughts and our desires. As to the Pride of Life, I am afraid that many Christians trickle to this third daughter of the First Adam by self-indulgence in dress, in expenses, in all sorts of showiness. Mark you, this Pride of Life, though the most respectable of the three, as people think, is as genuine a daughter of the Old Adam as is the Lust of the Flesh. I cannot imagine our Lord Jesus Christ dressing Himself so as to attract attention. . . . This daughter of the Old Adam is much set by in these days. She keeps the milliners' shops going, and she sends many a man into the bankruptcy court; and, alas! she is invited into many of our Christian circles, and thought right well of. (Ibid., pp. 150–51)

As Faithful is inclined to go with Old Adam he notices written on his forehead, "Put off the old man with his deeds." Each of us should have a conscience alert enough to realize that self-indulgence is not right for followers of Christ, who gave us the opposite example while here on earth. It is good for us to be reminded of the sin nature we have inherited from Adam the first, for it makes us value what Christ has done for us all the more to realize the hopeless, depraved nature from which we have been delivered and that our continued constant dependence on him is required for victory over Adam the first.

Leaving Adam the first behind, the two pilgrims discuss how Faithful was overtaken by Moses (the Law of God). As Jesus explained in the Sermon on the Mount, the Law of God is meant not only to en-compass the outward actions but to reach so far as the thoughts and intents of the heart. So strict, so pure, so spiritual is the holy Law of God that it will knock any man flat on the ground and leave him de-spairing. A comprehensive view of the Law and one's own sinful heart and actions can leave the believer discouraged. Yet this can lead to a humble dependence on Christ and to empathy for other believers. What gratitude we should have for Christ's nail-pierced hands, which alone can rescue. Only hard-hearted, blind fools will place their confidence in their meager attempts to obey the Law for their justification.

In the Valley of Humiliation Faithful met Discontent, an enemy with whom he reasoned and of whom he got the better. Christians may at first think that they may avoid the disdain that loyal adher-ence to Christianity brings. And thus discontentment may set in when they experience the consequent lose of offended friends and the worldly degradation. They may question if the cost of going against the carnal flesh and the loss of the "treasures" of this world are worth it. Faithful carefully considered all this and prevailed over the dis-content that springs from pride, arrogance, self-conceit, and a desire for worldly glory, riches, and pleasure. He correctly chose, like Pa-tience, the future reward and honor that comes from God.

Faithful's next encounter was with bold-faced Shame. Shame's objections to religion were countered by Faithful's thoughtful rea-soning, for he knew that what God says is best. Being ashamed of the things of God is a very powerful enemy to Christ's glory and the soul's well-being. It is better to grab Shame by the throat and make a bold stand than to cower before him, dreading the loss of any supposed earthly prestige. Christ has said that whoever is ashamed of him be-fore men he will be ashamed of before the Father (Mark 8:38). Of this crafty villain, Shame, Alexander Whyte states:

> In the present disorder of our souls, we are all acutely ashamed of many things that are not the proper objects of shame at all; while, on the other hand, we feel no shame at all at multitudes of things that are really most blameworthy, dishonorable, and contemptible. We are ashamed of things in our lot and in our circumstances that, if we only knew it, are our opportunity and our honor; we are ashamed of things that are the clear will and the immediate dispensation of Almighty God. (*First Series Bunyan Characters*, p. 171)

Shame does indeed get quite a bit of help from our fallen nature. Oh, let us cry for boldness to affirm our best friend, Jesus.

After Faithful recounts his story, we are introduced to Talkative. Of this tall man Cheever says:

> A professor of religion by the tongue, but not in the life, a hearer of the word, but not a doer, a great disgrace to religion, and in the description of the common people, a saint abroad, and a devil at home. But he was a great talker "of things heavenly or things earthly; things moral or things evangelical; things sacred or things profane; . . . or things circumstantial:—provided that all be done to profit." Faithful was much taken with this man. What a brave companion have we got, said he to Christian! Surely this man will make a very excellent pilgrim. Christian, who knew him well, related his parentage and character, and afterwards Faithful proceeded, according to Christian's directions, to converse with Talkative in such a way upon the subject of religion, as very soon proved what he was in reality, and delivered them of his company. (*Lectures on the Pilgrim's Progress*, pp. 360–61)

It is seen to be true that Talkative has a heart which is a stranger to grace, for he has no love of or power to practice what he preaches. True grace in the heart manifests itself in a godly life (obedience to the will of God), which brings glory to God. When no remorse, only defensiveness, is shown when error is exposed, we do well to heed the apostolic advice, "From such withdraw thyself." We do scandalous professors' souls no good by accepting them into church membership when their lives do not back up their words. Their actions cause nonbelievers to point at them and say, "See what a bunch of hypocrites these Christians are," which brings disgrace on Christ's bride, the church. By withdrawing from such Talkatives, we refuse to help them continue to carry on their deception of themselves, thus leaving them to self-examination, which we hope will bring them to be ashamed of their inconsistencies and to seek Christ.

L•E•S•S•O•N
6
The Temptations of Vanity Fair

Barbour and Company, Inc. 1985, pp. 95–110
Discovery House *New Pilgrim's Progress* with notes, pp. 104–18
Moody *Pilgrim's Progress in Today's English*, pp. 87–98
Moody Classic Edition, pp. 96–111
Revell Spire Book, pp. 78–90
Whitaker House 1981 Edition, pp. 102–16

Questions for Discussion or Reflection

Christian and Faithful again encounter Evangelist on the Way. They give him a cordial welcome and express their gratitude to him for his kindness and labors for their eternal good. Warned by Evangelist of a difficult time to come in Vanity Fair, they press forward in their journey. Christian and Faithful are easily identified as different at the Fair and are persecuted for their pursuit of Truth. A most despicable trial ensues, and a verdict is rendered in accordance with the judgments of the ungodly men of Vanity Fair.

1. Christian now meets Evangelist for the third time. Do you remember his first and second meetings with Christian? Describe them.

2. How do Christian and Faithful show their continued love and friendship for Evangelist?

3. Evangelist asks Christian and Faithful two questions. What are they, and what do you learn about Evangelist from these questions?

4. Evangelist gives Christian and Faithful five exhortations. What are they?

5. Christian asks Evangelist to tell them things that might happen to them and also how they might resist and overcome them. What are some of the things he describes?

6. Why do you think Vanity Fair is given such a name?

7. Bunyan describes the merchandise sold at this fair by listing many items. What are some of these items, and what types of sins do they represent?

How are Christians today caught up in these same types of sin?

8. Explain the meaning of this sentence: "But as in other fairs, some one commodity is as the chief of all the fair, so the ware of Rome

and her merchandize is greatly promoted in this Fair: Only our English nation, with some others, have taken a dislike thereat."

9. Why were the people in the town of Vanity moved and in a hubbub when Christian and Faithful entered?

10. Has there ever been an incident in your life like Christian and
Faithful's experience when the people of Vanity Fair "took them and
beat them and besmeared them with dirt and then put them into a
Cage, that they might be made a Spectacle to all the men of the Fair"?

11. How did Christian and Faithful respond to their persecution?

What were the responses of the men of Vanity Fair to their actions?

12. When Christian and Faithful were in the cage, how did they comfort each other?

13. What are some comments made by Judge Hate-Good that indi-
cate that his name is appropriate?

"If you lay your ear close enough to your own heart, you will sometimes hear something of that same hiss with which that human ser-
pent sentenced to torture to death the men and women who would
not submit to his command. The same savage laughter also will sometimes all but escape your lips as you think of how your enemy has
been made to suffer . . . the very same hell-broth . . . is in all our hearts

also" (Whyte, *First Series Bunyan Characters*, p. 195). Are there any areas of your own heart that resemble the character of Judge Hate-Good?

14. Three witnesses appear at the trial. Name them.

Sum up each of their testimonies briefly.

How does Faithful respond to their testimonies?

15. After reading the names of the jurors, what did you think the verdict would be for Faithful?

Have you ever acted like any of the jurors? Which one (or ones), and how?

16. What six things are done to Faithful?

17. How is Faithful the real victor in this situation?

18. Were there any parts, themes, or people in this section that you did not understand? Perhaps the group can help clarify them.

Summary and Applications

Christian and Faithful pass through a wilderness, a passage made easy by their soul-invigorating conversation about Christ and his dealings with them in love. We would do well to follow their example, for such thoughts can change our tedious or difficult times into pleasant paths as we look back on God's gracious acts toward us. What we talk about with our Christian friends often shows where our affections lie. Choose your friends with care, and "be much with those who are much with God . . . make those your companions on earth, who will be your companions in heaven" (Spurgeon, *Pictures from Pilgrim's Progress*, pp. 169–70).

Bunyan suitably places a third meeting with Evangelist here in the story. As they approach Vanity Fair, our pilgrims will be exposed to persecution, which they should expect, considering the hostility the world often shows towards true pilgrims. Timid believers are often tempted to retreat from the world, thus avoiding such ill treatment. But to neglect the active service and public situations to which God often calls us for the sake of a quiet, safe life is disobedience. We should expect and prepare for trials by seeking good instruction in the Word and by studying it diligently.

Well received are the words of Evangelist, who had first directed both Christian and Faithful to Christ, even though they had not seen each other often for various reasons. Evangelist shows himself to be a faithful minister as he inquires about the prosperity of their souls and about their pilgrimage thus far.

> How they rejoiced again to meet Evangelist, and listen to his encouraging and animating exhortations, of which, as they were now near the great town of Vanity Fair, they would stand in special need. Indeed, it was partly for the purpose of forewarning them of what they were to meet with there, and to exhort them, amidst all persecutions, to quit themselves like men, that Evangelist now came to them. His voice, so solemn and deep, yet so inspiring and animating, sounded like the tones of a trumpet on the eve of battle. (Cheever, *Lectures on the Pilgrim's Progress*, p. 361)

Evangelist instructs Christian and Faithful to be steadfast in faith, joyful in hope, and watchful over their hearts and to abound in the work of the Lord, all of which are especially necessary in the town that the two are about to visit. Evangelist tells them that most difficult times and martyrdom await in Vanity Fair. We should be ever mindful that we are not to find our satisfaction and rest in this world.

Christian and Faithful were indeed thankful to persistent Evangelist for his cautions, exhortations, and encouragements, which were helpful to them when the time came for their faith to be tested by the cruel treatment they received at Vanity Fair.

The view we have had thus far of our pilgrims' journey in this allegory has centered on the secret internal spiritual conflicts of the soul. We now enter Vanity Fair, which represents the various external conflicts a Christian must face. The seductive allurements of this world are presented in a tangible, visible form, and we see how real pilgrims conduct themselves among the various temptations of this fair. Here Bunyan describes the sharp contrast that exists between believers and nonbelievers and how believers are regarded and treated by the ungodly men of this world. Followers of Christ are sure to be called by all kinds of derogatory names when they take a stand for biblical moral standards. The names and responses met with go something like this: "What a prude! How narrow and unloving!" They tell us not to be so stiff, to loosen up: "What fun you are missing!" Nonetheless, in Scripture the Christian is depicted as one who lives above the world, who is dead to it and walks through it as a stranger and alien traveling to "the city . . . whose architect and builder is God" (Hebrews 11:10).

Christian and Faithful did not shop at the fair, for they had found true, lasting joy and satisfaction, which were not to be had at Vanity Fair.

> The happiest state of a Christian is the holiest state. As there is most heat nearest to the sun, so there is most happiness nearest to Christ. No Christian enjoys comfort when his eyes are fixed on vanity. I do not blame ungodly men for rushing to their pleasures. Let them have their fill. That is all they have to enjoy, but Christians must seek their delights in a higher sphere than the insipid frivolities of the world. Vain pursuits are dangerous to renewed souls. (Spurgeon, *Pictures*, p. 161)

Such a wide variety of merchandise is on display at the fair! There are all kinds of seductive allurements such as houses, lands, silver, gold, pearls, precious stones, and what not. But it is puzzling why anyone would spend so much time and attention in the pursuit and acquisition of inanimate objects (i.e., cars, houses, furniture, etc.), which are unable to respond in love to their great efforts. Often people have to slight time spent on relationships (at church, at home, and with God) in their mad pursuit of the vain things of this world, which will decay while those things which are eternal are given last place in their lives. Do we spend too much of our time on things that are good (in their proper place) but miss the best? We are instructed in the deceitfulness of riches when we see that men are *owned* by the things they have accumulated and pass their days in vain showiness.

Other fine wares displayed are earthly honors, preferments, and titles that swell our egos and heads. How hollow do they become for sincere believers who are careless of man's esteem and who strive after holiness (the Christian's true glory and honor)! The response of sound converts to achievements and work well done is "We are unworthy slaves; we have done only that which we ought to have done" (Luke 17:10). Also on display are the wares of pleasure and delights of all sorts.

> It is the sweetness of sin that makes it the more dangerous. Satan never sells his poisons naked; he always gilds them before he vends them. Beware of pleasures. Many of them are innocent and healthful, but many are destructive. It is said that where the most beautiful cacti grow, there the most venomous serpents lurk. It is so with sin. Your fairest pleasures will harbor your grossest sins. Take care! Cleopatra's asp was introduced in a basket of flowers. . . . He [Satan] gives to each of us the offer of our peculiar joy; he tickleth us with pleasures, that he may lay hold of us. (Ibid., p. 164)

"So the ware of Rome and her merchandise is greatly promoted in the fair" is a reference to the doctrines of the Roman Catholic Church. Remembering how recent the Reformation was in our author's time will help us to understand this statement. He declares that the merchandise (doctrine) of this church is "greatly promoted in this fair." And what a proud, unscriptural doctrine it is that barters with God and presumes to purchase entrance into heaven by good works and obedience, thus meriting heaven and justification and so exalting man and debasing the gracious work, glory, and honor of Christ. How sad is it that these wares of Rome are still being sold!

Bunyan gives us a most picturesque description of the wicked world in which we live. How alluring her wares can be! And, as John Gulliver states, "How many, though they profess to be pilgrims, have never yet set one foot out of this fair, but live in it all the year round! They walk according to the course of this world. Eph 2:2. . . . You cannot be a pilgrim, if you are not delivered from this world and its vanities; for if you love the world, if it has your supreme affections, the love of God is not in you. I John 2:15" (*The Complete Works of John Bunyan*, p. 132). Those who have nothing in their lives to distinguish them from the rest of the world have no reason to conclude that they are new creatures in Christ. Conformity to the world pollutes our morals and our souls, and compromise with the world and double-mindedness are not the example set by the Christians' commander in chief. Be careful what you do. Don't stray too close to sin, for it will suck you down as surely as quicksand.

> An unholy church! it is useless to the world, and of no esteem among men. It is an abomination, hell's laughter, heaven's abhorrence. The worst evils which have ever come upon the world have been brought upon her by an unholy church. O Christian, the vows of the Lord are upon you. You are God's priest: act as such. You are God's king: reign over your lusts. You are God's chosen: do not associate with Belial. Heaven is your portion: live like a heavenly spirit. So shall you prove that you have true faith in Jesus, for there cannot be faith in the heart unless there be holiness in the life. (Spurgeon, *Pictures*, p. 170)

All attempts at compromise in matters of truth and holiness are founded upon error. How different would our thoughts and actions be if we were to heed the following comments by Spurgeon:

> Remember, O Christian, that thou art a son of the King of kings. Therefore keep thyself unspotted from the world. Soil not the fingers which are soon to sweep celestial strings; let not those eyes become the windows of lust which are soon to see the King in His beauty; let not those feet be defiled in miry places, which are soon to walk the golden streets; let not those hearts be filled with pride and bitterness which are ere long to be filled with heaven, and to overflow with ecstatic joy. (Ibid., p. 166)

Christian and Faithful cause the town to be in a hubbub, for they are clothed in different raiment (Christ's robes of righteousness), their speech is the language of Canaan (spiritual conversation), and they are unimpressed by the wares of the fair. What Christian and Faithful seek to buy, the truth, is not available at Vanity Fair, for the wicked world is under the delusion cast by the Father of Lies and is deceived by his falsehoods. Because of their pursuit of the truth found in Christ, Satan stirs up the world against believers. It is a sure fact of this present age that if we live a godly, gracious life we will not escape persecution. And so poor Christian and Faithful are dragged off by the men of Vanity Fair, who are astonished and indignant at the disinterest the pilgrims show to worldly things—such things as would interfere with the will of God. As the two are examined and declare their principles, the rage of the men of the fair is only increased and Christian and Faithful are beaten and then placed in a cage. Though beaten and despised, they do not lose heart, for their attitude is that which Luther had when he said: "Joy in the Lord is more injurious to Satan's empire than anything. Come, let us sing a psalm and spite the devil" (ibid., p. 187). Those who do not stoop to giving "railing for railing" when they are unjustly persecuted, but endure sufferings in a proper manner, honor God with their behavior. They heap coals on their tormentors' heads, and their quiet, submissive attitude pricks the cruelest, most hardened consciences. God will bring comfort to them as they follow the example Christ gave when He said, "Father, forgive them; for they know not what they do" (Luke 23:34, KJV).

After a time, Christian and Faithful are brought forth to stand trial. Bunyan no doubt was well acquainted with such trials from his own life and times. The indictment was as follows: "That they were enemies to, and disturbers of their trade: that they had made commotions and divisions in the town, and had won a party to their own most dangerous opinions, in contempt of the law of their prince." Could such an indictment be brought against you? The names of the characters Bunyan uses here are meant to expose the real reason why holy believers are on trial in the world even today. The corrupt principles of the human heart are shown in Judge Hate-Good, Envy, Pick-thank, Superstition, and the jurors (Mr. Malice, Mr. Love-lust, Mr. Live-loose, Mr. High-mind, Mr. Cruelty, Mr. Hate-light, etc.) and are expressed in hatred of God, his holy character, his wisdom, and all who serve him. Judge Hate-Good's court illustrates that the more godly Christians are, the more they will be hated for it. Such good people go against and expose by their holy behavior the immorality, selfishness, pride, and evil of the unbeliever's pursuits. The holy, chaste light of goodness is a constant irritation to the wicked, and they seek to get rid of the light that is shining on their dark lives.

Envy is the first witness to appear; he charges Faithful with disloyalty to their country, customs, and rulers. Envy is the very disposition of the Devil and very much a part of our fallen nature. "What an utterly and abominably evil passion is envy which is awakened not by bad things but by the best things! That another man's talents, attainments, praises, rewards should kindle it, and that the blame, the depreciation, the hurt that another man suffers should satisfy it— what a piece of very hell must that be in the human heart!" (Whyte, *First Series*, pp. 95–96). Superstition, one who rests in forms and rites but does not worship God in spirit and truth, gives an accurate account of Faithful's assessment of the religion of the fair (i.e., that the merchants are vain, still in their sins, and sure to be damned). The last witness to come forth is Pickthank. A pickthank is a man who has no religious principles but will assume the garb of whatever party best suits his interests and advances him in the world. We should desire the testimony he gave against Faithful to be true of us also.

Faithful finally speaks in his own defense. He takes divine revelation as his standard of life and conduct; if this is unpopular, so be it. And in response to Superstition he says that he will do nothing that is not the express warrant of Scripture; he will do only what is found in the Bible to be profitable to eternal life. And as for Mr. Pickthank and the friends he represents, Faithful points out that their vile lusts make them fit for hell and Faithful stands with Christ, whom the world hated, because he testified of it that its works were evil (John 7:7).

Judge Hate-Good instructs the jury regarding cases of the past and the anti-Christian precedents they have set. From the names of the jurors, it is easy to guess the verdict. May we also be convicted of the same crimes as those Faithful committed and receive a verdict such as is worthy of true pilgrims.

Faithful's ordeal was not in vain, for "the martyrdom of Faithful had kindled a light in Vanity Fair that would not easily be put out, and many there were that by his example would themselves, as Hopeful did, become pilgrims. So, by the death of one [Faithful] to bear testimony to the truth, many were affected by that testimony, whose hearts might otherwise have remained hardened to the end of life" (Cheever, *Lectures*, p. 380). Faithful's sure, eternal reward awaits him as a chariot whisks him off to the Celestial Gate to meet the king under whose banner he has so valiantly served.

L·E·S·S·O·N
7
Hopeful Joins Christian

Barbour and Company, Inc. 1985, pp. 110–35
Discovery House *New Pilgrim's Progress* with notes, pp. 120–41
Moody *Pilgrim's Progress in Today's English*, pp. 99–118
Moody Classic Edition, pp. 111–37
Revell Spire Book, pp. 90–110
Whitaker House 1981 Edition, pp. 117–41

Questions for Discussion or Reflection

After leaving Vanity Fair, Christian is given another excellent companion in Hopeful. As they strike up a conversation with By-ends, they are exposed to his fatal and soul-deceiving error of being double-minded in all his ways. Christian and Hopeful withdraw from By-ends when they perceive his condition. By-ends then finds three new companions with whom he makes an agreeable friendship. They attempt to unite the love of money with the love of Christ. Though God graciously preserves Christian and Hopeful as they pass by Demas and the hill Lucre, the two pilgrims trust their own wisdom (make a sinful choice) and fall into the hands of the giant named Despair.

1. Hopeful now joins Christian, "entering into a brotherly covenant." What do you think was involved in this brotherly covenant?

If you were to enter into a covenant with a fellow Christian, what would be included in your covenant?

2. After leaving Vanity Fair, Hopeful and Christian meet By-ends. How would you describe this character?

3. By-ends tries to go two ways at once. He has two goals: to be religious and to hold on to the world at the same time. Why is this impossible (Luke 16:13)?

4. By-ends says that he differs in two small points "in Religion from those of the stricter sort." What are the two small points?

How do Christians with this type of philosophy act today?

5. How does By-ends reveal his hypocritical character when he tells Hopeful and Christian how he got his nickname?

6. Christian and Hopeful forsake By-ends. What three men are his new companions?

These men had been school-fellows. Who was their schoolmaster, and what had he taught them?

Have you ever met a graduate from this school?

7. How does By-ends describe Christian and Hopeful?

8. After By-ends and his companions have convinced themselves by both Scripture and reason that Christian and Hopeful are in error, By-ends propounds a question for their diversion. Basically, the question is this: If a preacher or layman has a chance to gain an advantage by appearing more zealous in some points of religion than he has previously been, can he not do so and still be honest? Money-love offers an answer in the affirmative. What are the four reasons he gives regarding the minister?

What are the three reasons he gives regarding the tradesman?

9. How does Christian respond to the question when Mr. Hold-the-World propounds it to him?

10. What four types of people does Christian say will believe the argument By-ends and his companions have used? Describe how each of them illustrates the point he is making.

11. Christian summarizes with a fifth point. What is his summary in your own words? Give an example.

12. Leaving By-ends and his companions speechless, Christian and Hopeful quickly get over a delicate plain called Ease and come to a little hill called Lucre. Who was Demas in the Bible?

What does Demas invite them to do, and why does Christian refuse?

Have you ever accepted Demas's invitation? When?

13. Christian says that he knows Demas's great-grandfather and father. Who were they and what was their fate (2 Kings 5:20)?

14. By-ends and his companions encounter an uncertain end at Demas's beckoning and are never seen in the Way again. However, on the other side of the plain Christian and Hopeful see something. What is it, and what do they ascertain is the meaning of it?

Hopeful wonders that he is not like this object. Why?

Men who sin in the full knowledge of the punishment are compared to what kind of people?

15. After a pleasant interlude by the river of God, Christian and Hopeful set out on their pilgrimage again. The river and the Way part. Why do they wish for a better way?

How do they illustrate Proverbs 14:12?

16. When we are tempted to sin, as Christian and Hopeful are in stepping out of the Way, Satan says: "Go ahead and sin. God loves you,

and repentance is an easy thing." However, once we have sinned, Satan's tune changes and he says, "What a miserable sinner you are. Repentance is impossible. God will never forgive you." How do Doubting Castle and the giant Despair illustrate the truth of the above statements?

Why is it that we seldom read about such despair over sin in our day?

Do you agree with the following statement? "Despair is not good, but it is infinitely better than indifference. It is a common saying and an observation in divinity, that where despair has slain its thousands, presumption has slain its ten thousands. The agonies of the former are indeed more terrible, but the securities of the latter are far more fatal" (Whyte, *First Series Bunyan Characters*, p. 232).

What other doctrinal truths are illustrated by Doubting Castle and the giant Despair? Pick out several of them to share with the group.

How do Christian and Hopeful finally escape? Have you ever escaped the giant Despair by these means? Name a few such instances.

Summary and Applications

Our dreamer now sees Christian joined by Hopeful. As is often the case in the Christian life, as one friend is taken away, God graciously grants the believer another blessed companion. Hopeful had learned the hard way that the toys and trinkets offered at Vanity Fair could not satisfy a heart that was made for God to fill. Hopeful's heart was so empty that the words and behavior of Christian and Faithful caught his attention and he decided to venture forth with Christian. They now enter into a brotherly covenant. Though Bunyan does not give details of what was involved in this covenant, might we imagine that the two agreed to have one goal—the advancement of God's Kingdom and his glory? We also see as we journey on that godly advice was exchanged between them and that they stirred up one another's affections as they talked about the God they adored. And would not there be agreement to times of prayer together during which they would go hand in hand before God's throne of grace? Also, we will witness evidence of the fact that they had agreed to confront each other with the sin they perceived in each other's lives—a very much neglected act in Christian fellowships today. Thomas Shepard further encourages us to adopt this idea of brotherly covenanting with these words: "Enter into covenant and brotherly promise to exhort one another, as David and Jonathan. . . . Some may in church fellowship be more nearly knit than others, to call one another to account, to tell one another their fears, to know of one another their progress. Canst thou not give an account to man? How wilt thou give an account to God of it?" (*The Parable of the Ten Virgins*, p. 382). So we see the benefit of Christian friendship, for as "iron sharpens iron, so one man [Christian] sharpens another [Hopeful]" (Proverbs 27:17).

The pilgrims quickly overtake By-ends, who has been going before them. "Bunyan uses all his great gifts of insight and sense and humor and scorn so as to mark unmistakably the road and to guide the progress of his reader's soul to God, his chiefest end and his everlasting portion" (Whyte, *First Series Bunyan Characters*, p. 215). In sharp contrast, By-ends has missed the road to his soul's chief end and everlasting portion, God, by exalting himself to that position. "By-ends was so called because he was full of low, mean, selfish motives, and of nothing else. All that this wretched creature did, he did with a single eye to himself. The best things that he did became bad things in his self-seeking hands. His very religion stank in those men's nostrils who knew what was in his heart" (ibid., p. 217). His name denotes not only his character but also the nature of the religion he professes. His religion is used to gain friends, fortune, and applause, but if persecution should arise because of strict adherence to the Word, he will deny his supposed profession of faith every time. By-end's motto was always "What's in it for me?"

Before we point our fingers and shake our heads at despicable By-ends, perhaps we should point our fingers back at ourselves and examine our own hearts. As Richard Hooker says of Christians: "Even in the good things that we do, how many defects are there intermingled! For God in that which is done respecteth especially the mind and intention of the doer. Cut off, then, all those things wherein we have regarded our own glory, those things which we do to please men, or to satisfy our own liking, those things which we do with any by-respect, and not sincerely and purely for the love of God, and a small score will serve for the number of our righteous deeds" (ibid.). While we are very adept at seeing sin in other's lives, we are often stone-blind to many of the sins in our own lives. We would do well to do as Mr. Whyte recommends.

> Witness against, judge, and execute yourselves, and that especially because of your by-aims and by-ends. Take up the touchstone of truth and lay it upon your most secret heart. Do not be afraid to discover how double-minded and deceitful your heart is. Hunt your heart down. Track it to its most secret lair. Put its true name, and continue to put its true name, upon the main motive of your life. Extort an answer . . . from the inner man of the heart, to the torturing question as to what is his treasure, his hope, his deepest wish, his daily dream. Watch not against any outward enemy, keep all your eyes and all your ears to your own thoughts. God keeps His awful eye on your thoughts. His eye goes at every glance to that great depth in you. . . . Go as deep as God goes, and you will be a wise man. (Ibid., p. 220)

Oh, how deep down in our hearts can those ulterior motives hide! Until we learn to serve Christ and love him because "he is altogether lovely" and not only for the benefits we receive from Him, we have some of By-ends in ourselves.

How different is Christ! He never had to be ashamed of any of his motives. Such things as concern over what he would wear, the honor he would receive for doing a certain deed, or the power and praise he might obtain were foreign to his pure heart and holy nature. All these things that men strive so desperately for gave him cause to feel only indifference or contempt. Christ's goal and aim was to please his Father by doing his will. This was his meat and his drink; this was better than anything the world could offer. Though Christ was tempted to do things with wrong motives, he never yielded to these temptations. O Lord, enable us to imitate Christ and forget our self-centered desires, seeking only your glory in all that we do. Help us to examine our hearts to see if there is any of the character of this By-ends in us, and by your power free us from this wretched trait. Enable us to seek you for your grace and truth and not for loaves and fish or with other unsacred motives. "Until you begin to watch your own thoughts, and to watch them especially in their aims and their ends, you will have no idea what that moral and spiritual life is that all God's saints live; that life that Christ lived, and which He summons you all to enter henceforth upon" (ibid., pp. 220–21).

After they have talked with By-ends for a while Christian and Hopeful part company with him. When believers have full proof that someone's profession of faith is false, they must reprove such a person and then, if this has no effect, withdraw themselves from that person. Looking back, the pilgrims see By-ends team up with a trio of former schoolmates, Mr. Hold-the-World, Mr. Money-love, and Mr. Save-all. Their schoolmaster, Mr. Gripe-man, had taught them the art of getting by putting on the guise of religion. The dialogue that follows is a humorous satire exposing their selfish attempts to serve God and love money at the same time.

By-ends proposes the question, "If a minister or a businessman has a chance to get ahead by appearing more zealous for religion than he really is, can he not do this and still be considered honest?" We then witness worldly wisdom and logic not to be outdone by Satan himself. How dangerous are evil motives hidden under the guise of a good cause! So true is the saying, "The motive is everything; it makes the man." These men, however, are so confident of their answer and argument that they next put the question to Christian and Hopeful, expecting to puzzle and defeat them. Christian completely amazes them by declaring that only heathens, hypocrites, devils, and witches could be of such an opinion and giving clear proof of this from Scripture. And what has Scripture to say of these schoolmates and their talk? "The love of money is the root of all evil" (1 Timothy 6:10, KJV), and "a covetous man is an idolater" (Colossians 3:5). And Christ has said, "You cannot serve God and mammon" (Luke 16:13). We are only stewards of what God has entrusted to us, all of which is to be used as he directs, not for hoarding or worldly indulgence. When our motives are revealed by the light of God's brilliant holiness on the last day, how many of our supposed good deeds will be found to have been less than honorable and based on carefully concealed self-interest and greed?

Christian and Hopeful quickly get over a plain called Ease and come to a little hill called Lucre. A little off the road stands Demas, who calls to them to turn aside. Often outward peace and prosperity cause Christians to be tempted to seek riches and earthly honors, which are far from their thoughts in more difficult times because they then draw near to God in great dependence. Hopeful desires to dig for treasure, but Christian acts as a faithful friend by pointing out the snare and hindrance that treasure is to pilgrims in the Way. Covetousness and mad pursuit after riches is idolatry as surely as bowing down to Baal is, and how few there are who will reprimand a fellow believer for such and inform him of Christ's warning (Luke 7:13)! We ought also to heed this scriptural caution: "It is easier for a camel to go through the eye of a needle, than for a rich man to enter the kingdom of God" (Matthew 19:24). On this verse Coleridge muses, "Often as the motley reflexes of my experience move in long processions of manifold groups before me, the distinguished and world-honored company of Christian Mammonists appear to the eye of my imagination as a drove of camels heavily laden, yet all at full speed, and each in the confident expectation of passing through the eye of the needle, without stop or halt, both beasts and baggage!" (Cheever, *Lectures on the Pilgrim's Progress*, p. 390). We would do well to ask ourselves, "What will a man be profited, if he gains the whole world, and forfeits his soul?" (Matthew 16:26). Yes, the whole world may be gained if you are willing to barter your soul, but at what cost? From the crazed thinking of Vanity Fair may we be delivered!

The fate of By-ends and his cohorts unfolds as their double-mindedness in trying to unite the love of money with the love of Christ fails and "at first beck" from Demas they go over, never to be seen in the Way again.

After they take a warning from the old monument of Lot's wife, the pilgrims come to the river of God, beside which they are greatly refreshed as they eat from the trees, drink from the river, and relax for several days and nights. As they continue, the river and the Way part "for a while" as the path becomes rough. Christian spies a meadow "on the left hand of the road" and suggests that they take what seems to be an easier way. To get over into By-path Meadow they must go over a stile, that is, they must quit Christ's protection and trust in their own wisdom. By-path Meadow represents shrinking back from the hardness of the pilgrimage and a departure from its duties. It is difficult to believe that the two pilgrims could have such a sudden fall from the very gate of heaven (the river of life) to the very gate of hell (Doubting Castle). This should be a warning to those who have had great joy and spiritual edification to beware of seeking after spiritual enjoyment rather than usefulness and growth in grace by active discipline and duty. It is possible that spiritual enjoyments themselves may become a snare, making the pilgrim unwilling to separate from such a blessed quietness of life when the true pilgrimage leads to a rougher road. Sooner or later Doubting Castle will be the prison, and the giant Despair the keeper of all those who turn aside from Christ to trust in themselves in any way. We should remember, however, that Doubting Castle is not the will of God for believers but the effect of sin and unbelief. Our pilgrims have made several errors: they have discontentedly desired a better, easier way; they have looked at the easier way; and then they have climbed over the stile. Does this remind you of a scene in the Garden of Eden?

Caught by the giant Despair, Christian and Hopeful are cast into his dungeon. The giant Despair personifies what may come upon us because of sin, the regret we have for sin committed and the sense of sin that burdens the conscience. This part of *Pilgrim's Progress* shows us the depth of misery into which sin may plunge the Christian and also the depth to which the mercy of God in Christ may reach. On the pilgrim's arrival in this pitiful condition Cheever comments:

> Some men enter by unbelief, and whatever state of mind or habit of sin shuts out the Savior, is sure to bring a man there at once. Some men enter by pride and self-righteousness; if a man trusts in his own merits, instead of the blood and righteousness of Christ for justification. . . . Some men enter this castle by habits of self-indulgence, some by particular cherished sins, some by dallying with temptations, some by sudden falling into deep sins, some by neglect of watchfulness and prayer, some by a gradual creeping coldness and stupor in the things of religion, the dangerous spirit of slumber not being guarded against and resisted. Some get into this prison by natural gloom and despondency of mind, of which Satan takes an advantage. . . . Neglect of God's Word will take men to this prison, leaning to one's own understanding, and distorted views of divine truth. . . . Some get in by spiritual sins, others by sensual; some by conformity to the world; some by the pressure of business, others by the cares of life and the deceitfulness of riches. . . . Alas! how many ways there are

of getting into this gloomy prison! Oh, if Christ be not always with the soul, or if at any time it go astray from him, or if its reliance be on any thing whatever but his mercy, his blood, his grace, then is it near the gloom of this Dungeon. (*Lectures*, pp. 393–94)

John Bunyan suffered all his life from an easily wounded conscience; therefore, he was very familiar with Doubting Castle and the giant Despair. As we consider the Bible and particularly the Psalms, we learn that the holier a man is, the more liable he is to the assaults of doubt, fear, and even despair. Though despair is not good, it is infinitely better than indifference to sin. So deep was David's sense of sin, so high were his views of God's holiness and justice, and so full of sorrow was his wounded heart that he pled with God, "Cast me not away from thy presence; and take not thy holy spirit from me. Restore unto me the joy of thy salvation; and uphold me with thy free spirit" (Psalm 51:11–12, KJV). David saw clearly how awful it was to grieve the Holy Spirit by sin so that he withdraws. David knew from personal experience that the Holy Spirit is the only true Comforter. Though precious promises are contained in Scripture, we can gain no comfort from them except through the Spirit, for the Word and the Spirit work together for our deliverance.

After being held captive from Wednesday to Saturday, at about midnight the pilgrims begin to pray. When believers turn to prayer in Doubting Castle, deliverance is close at hand. A little before daybreak Christian remembers the key in his bosom, which is called Promise. The precious promises in Scripture are indeed the key to the life of faith and deliverance through Christ. We observe here how doubt and despair rob Christians of their courage, reason, and grace and keep them prisoner, but how one single thought of the love, power, and grace of God in Christ frees them from this dungeon.

Though the pilgrims had sinned greatly in leaning to their own understanding, God had graciously taught them some valuable lessons from this bitter experience. They had learned never to depart from God's Way and anything that he desired them to go through, to value the light of God's countenance and to distrust themselves more thoroughly. They had been taught the dreadful evil of sin and sin's consequences; they had seen their weakness and Christ's strength and that the only way of deliverance was by casting themselves totally on Christ. It would be beneficial for us to remember these truths as well.

L•E•S•S•O•N
8
Rest for the Soul at the Delectable Mountains

Barbour and Company, Inc. 1985, pp. 135–40
Discovery House *New Pilgrim's Progress* with notes, pp. 143–47
Moody *Pilgrim's Progress in Today's English*, pp. 119–22
Moody Classic Edition, pp. 138–43
Revell Spire Book, pp. 110–14
Whitaker House 1981 Edition, pp. 142–47

Questions for Discussion or Reflection

After Christian and Hopeful leave Doubting Castle and the giant Despair, we are made aware that the Christian life is a continual series of ups and downs, prosperity and adversity, which Christians must go through on their way to heaven. All these experiences are brought about to conform us to the image of Christ. Hebrews 5:8 says that Christ learned obedience by the things that he suffered. Certainly if the Son of God learned in this way, we may expect the same. The two pilgrims now reach the Delectable Mountains, where they are "shown some wonders" by the four shepherds.

1. Various meanings have been applied to the Delectable Mountains. Some see them as representing nothing in particular other than a time of quiet rest. Others see these mountains as a picture of the local church. Still others say that the mountains represent the ministry of the Word of God by godly pastors and its effect on pilgrims. While

all these are good interpretations of the Delectable Mountains, might I add another possibility? The Puritans called the Sabbath a "market day for the soul." Could these mountains represent the Sabbath and all that Sabbath rest entails (i.e., a day set aside for instruction in Sunday school, for sitting under the preaching of godly ministers, and for meditation on Scripture and prayer)? If this is what they represent, how do the Delectable Mountains remind you of a market day for the soul?

time of rest, remembering & reflection, refreshment

2. What meaning would you ascribe to the Delectable Mountains? Explain why. *Sabbath - it encompasses all those things.*

3. Name the four shepherds. *Knowledge, Experience, Watchful & Sincere*

Their names imply what about the responsibilities of pastors to their flocks? *Knowledge = study/growth*
Experience = actively engaged w/God
Watchful = protector of flock
Sincere = authentic/truth in love

If you were asked to pick one of the shepherds for your pastor, which one would you pick? Give reasons for your choice.

Sincere

4. In the morning the shepherds call Christian and Hopeful to walk with them and show them four different places. Name the four places.

Error   *Doubting Castle*
Caution   *By-way to Hell*

Describe each place.

What truth is taught from each place?

5. When Christian and Hopeful are about to depart, what gifts and advice do the shepherds give them?

Summary and Applications

After escaping from the giant Despair, Christian and Hopeful have a refreshing and instructive time on the Delectable Mountains. Our two travelers would have reached these mountains sooner if Christian had not misled Hopeful, causing them to end up in Doubting Castle. What sadness and needless pain we often put ourselves and others through by our disobedience and sin!

Here they meet four shepherds. In the shepherds' names are found the traits of a godly minister. The first shepherd is Knowledge. Alexander Whyte says of him, "All his great talents were his Master's gift to him, his great attainments are all his own to lay out in his Master's service. . . . [These gifts of] understanding and memory and industry must all be sanctified by secret prayer many times every day, and then laid out every day in the instruction, impression, and comfort of his people" (*First Series Bunyan Characters*, pp. 240–41). However, a truly great minister will have the highest knowledge, a thorough knowledge of the Bible and thus of himself. From this knowledge then he will feed his sheep, showing them the holiness of God and the depravity of the human heart. His soul will be laid bare as he preaches earnestly because of the burden God has laid upon his soul.

Secondly, there is Experience. An elderly pastor once said, "Even God himself cannot inspire an experience." It is true that by its very nature an experience has to be undergone. A pastor is able to speak with absolute authority about God's comfort and the strength of his everlasting arms after going through a difficult time in which the existence of these attributes has been proved by experience. It is knowledge that has been tried and tested in the crucible of God's furnace that enables a pastor to bring to life verses printed on a page, to send flaming arrows to pierce hard hearts. Blessed is the pastor who can speak with such authority on the basis of his own experience of God.

Watchful, the third shepherd, represents a good pastor, who is attentive over the souls of his congregation. His vigilance will be seen as he visits, instructs, and personally deals with his people. Richard Baxter, a watchful shepherd (pastor) of the 1600s, set a godly example as he catechized and visited every member of his congregation each year—and this was in addition to preaching several times a week and performing his vast daily writing labors. He shows us that it is not so much a lack of time but a lack of intention that hinders many in this area. Also, a watchful shepherd is able to detect wolves when they break in to do harm to the sheep, and he deals with them accordingly.

In the fourth shepherd, named Sincere, is represented the value of a minister who has pure, godly intentions. His sincerity towards God is seen in his holy living, and thus he is highly esteemed by his people. He is a transparent man who means what he says to his flock, having no ulterior motives. When he warns his people of the evil and damaging consequences of sin and of how deep in the heart it can hide, these cautions pierce the people's consciences, for they know that he warns them for their own good. He is patient with the weak, for he realizes that they injure themselves with their carelessness, and he remembers God's forbearance over the years concerning his own faults. He is a shepherd who has a right, sincere, and godly interest in and intention for his flock, and thus he is a skillful, safe guide to follow.

As we consider the fine characteristics of godly shepherds, may we also remember that, all that has been said of the shepherds should also be true of the sheep. May we be sheep who have sincere, pure motives and who ever keep watchful eyes upon ourselves as we look deep into our own souls, at the roots of our actions and beliefs, and continually ask God to enable us to keep our hearts clean. And may our head knowledge be combined with heart knowledge that will put genuine zeal and passion for God's honor and glory on display before the world.

The shepherds take Christian and Hopeful to four different places for their edification. The first, the hill of error, is made up of intricate speculations not backed up by Scripture and deceptive reasonings founded on human theories. These falsehoods lead men from the clear truths found in the Bible into dangerous and destructive errors, causing them to climb too high on loose gravel and unstable lookouts, to fall, and to be dashed to pieces.

Next the group climbs to the top of a mountain called Caution. We have a great need to gaze constantly from Mount Caution, to see what awful things have happened to others and to learn from their mistakes. As Christian and Hopeful gaze upon the blind men stumbling among the tombs, unable to get out, tears of thankfulness come to their eyes, for they realize that but for God's graciousness and mercy to them, they would be as these blind men.

They are next taken to a place in a bottom where they see a door in the side of a hill. When they open the door, they hear a rumbling noise like that of fire and the cry of the tormented. It is explained that this is a by-way to hell, a way that hypocrites enter. With sadness, we see how much some men and women can be exposed to the truth and yet in the end reject it because of the perverseness of their hearts and the bondage of their wills to sin. Should these examples not cause us to walk humbly, yet diligently, ever looking to Jesus, who is able to keep us from falling?

As we look back over these instructions the shepherds have given us, we may be tempted to say, if it is all up to God's mercy and grace to keep us from falling into error, why apply ourselves to the means of grace? Though it is true that we are ever held by God's mercy and grace, he has appointed means of which we are to avail ourselves for our spiritual growth and well-being. Perhaps this idea can be compared to sailing. A sailor desires to travel from one end of a lake to the other. He proceeds to carefully inspect his equipment, working to mend and fix it as necessary. He then raises the sails, but he will not be able to go anywhere unless God is pleased to send the wind. It is also a sure fact that his boat will not move if he has failed to prepare it properly for the wind. So it is with the Christian. He may read the Bible, pray, and sit under godly preaching, but if the Holy Spirit does not graciously illumine spiritual truth, there will be no spiritual growth. As Jonathan Edwards has so eloquently said, "The more you have of a rational knowledge of divine things, the more opportunity will there be, when the Spirit shall be breathed into your heart, to see the excellency of these things, and to taste the sweetness of them" (*The Works of Jonathan Edwards*, 2:162).

The pilgrims are next given a view of heaven from the hill called Clear. How thankful we should be to our pastors, who give us glimpses of heaven each Sunday and invite us to walk in the suburbs of the Celestial City with their clear teachings! Christian and Hopeful's view of the Celestial City is hampered by their shaking hands as they look through the glass of God's Word. Often our unbelief and fear, not to mention our constant gazing with love in the wrong direction, cause us to be unable to appreciate or to see clearly the beauty of all that awaits us as joint heirs with Christ of the everlasting kingdom of God.

On the Delectable Mountains pilgrims are given a chance to "have their souls catch up with their bodies" after a hectic, difficult, exhausting week. How we should prize and guard the Sabbath, which is to be a foretaste of heaven, and use it to worship God and nourish our eternal souls! As Christian and Hopeful depart, the shepherds give them those things which will aid them in their journey, as we shall soon observe.

L•E•S•S•O•N

9

Devious Travelers Confront Christian

Barbour and Company, Inc. 1985, pp. 140–65
Discovery House *New Pilgrim's Progress* with notes, pp. 147–69
Moody *Pilgrim's Progress in Today's English*, pp. 123–37
Moody Classic Edition, pp. 143–67
Revell Spire Book, pp. 114–35
Whitaker House 1981 Edition, pp. 148–73

Questions for Discussion or Reflection

Leaving the refreshing Delectable Mountains, our pilgrims meet a very brisk lad called Ignorance. Ignorance has come out of the country of Conceit but still observes many of its customs and traditions, believing that he can in some way contribute to his righteousness before God. Individuals such as Ignorance, Jesus calls thieves and robbers, for they rob him of the glory of his grace and trivialize the complete sufficiency of his atoning sacrifice. As Christian and Hopeful travel on, Christian relates a story about the robbery of a man named Little-Faith, from which we catch a glimpse of the seed of true faith, however weak, and learn a lesson in diligence and dependence on the grace that Christ bestows. Next our pilgrims meet the Flatterer. We observe that not only gospel hypocrites but also real disciples are sometimes led astray by delusions not examined in the light of Scripture, leading to self-righteousness and spiritual pride. Graciously rescued from the net of their error, Christian and Hopeful are

80

disciplined and go softly along the right way singing. A man with his back towards Zion comes up to them. This so-called seeker of twenty years proves to be another enemy of the cross. The pilgrims then come to the enchanted ground, and here they are inclined "to grow drowsy in soul," for upon these grounds all things go easily, smoothly, and well. Determined not to fall asleep, they manage their fellowship well and engage in a lively conversation.

1. The pilgrims meet Ignorance, from the country of Conceit. When Christian asks Ignorance on what he bases his hopes of heaven, how does Ignorance respond?

Have you ever had any experience with someone like Ignorance?

What did Christian and Hopeful decide would be the best way to witness to Ignorance?

2. Christian and Hopeful enter into a very dark lane. What do they see?

From the inscription on this man's back, what clue do you get as to how he deserved his fate?

3. Christian tells a story about a man by the name of Little-Faith. What do you think the following elements of the story represent? Little-Faith.

His bag of silver and spending money.

His jewels.

His certificate.

Mr. Faint-Heart.

Mr. Mistrust.

Mr. Guilt.

Great Grace.

4. How do the "three sturdy Rogues" work in the lives of Christians today as they did in the story of Little-Faith?

Whom were they afraid of?

5. How was Little-Faith able to keep his certificate?

6. Though Little-Faith was able to keep his certificate and jewels, why did he make little use of them?

7. Why was Little-Faith not able to sell his Jewels?

8. What person from Scripture is mentioned who was "so foiled and run down by these villains"?

9. "When therefore we hear that such Robberies are done on the King's Highway," what two things should we do?

10. Briefly, what is the meaning of this story?

11. After discussing the story of Little-Faith, Christian and Hopeful come to a place where they see a way "put itself into their Way." What happens next?

How does 2 Corinthians 11:13, 14 remind you of the first man they meet?

How could they have avoided the net?

Who rescues Christian and Hopeful, and how?

What means did he use to correct and caution them?

12. Next the pilgrims meet "a man with his back toward Zion." What is his name?

What advice does he give to Christian and Hopeful, and why does he give it?

When Christian says to Hopeful, "Is it true which this man hath said?" to test him, how does Hopeful respond to him?

13. Christian and Hopeful come to the enchanted ground. By the enchanted ground Bunyan is illustrating those periods in the Christian life when there is ease and little difficulty. There are no financial problems, good health is enjoyed, and there are harmonious relationships with friends and family. There are no major problems or afflictions. Hopeful wants to lie down and nap. Why will Christian not let him sleep?

What do you think happens when Christians sleep on the enchanted ground?

We learn to prize the company of good Christian friends as we consider the story of Christian and Hopeful in the enchanted ground. How does Christian suggest that they prevent drowsiness?

14. As Hopeful shares his testimony, several valuable insights are shared. What brought conviction of sin to him?

When he endeavored to mend his life by good works, why did Trouble come tumbling upon him again?

What caused Hopeful to believe Faithful's statement that he needed to "obtain the Righteousness of a man that never had sinned"?

What was Hopeful instructed to say when he went before the Mercy-Seat?

There are several key phrases in this prayer that make it theologically correct. What are they?

Do you see any difference between the typical way one is helped to receive Christ today and Hopeful's conversion experience?

How did Hopeful answer his own question, "but Lord, what is Believing?"

What effect did the revelation of Christ to Hopeful's soul have upon his spirit?

Summary and Applications

Going down the mountains, Christian and Hopeful meet a brisk lad from the country of Conceit, who is named Ignorance. It would be far better if none of us still breathed the air from his country, but sadly too many of us still do. So long as people think they can do anything towards making themselves righteous before God, their name is Ignorance and they are full of self-righteous conceit. Ignorance has based his hope of entrance into heaven on his own works and deeds and not on what Christ has done and the meritorious standing we receive from Christ's perfect work. Later we will have another encounter with Ignorance during which his theology will be further debated and we will finally see the awful disappointment that awaits him at the gates of the Celestial City because of his prideful, self-seeking, and self-exalting ways. When Christian and Hopeful see that Ignorance is wise in his own conceit, they leave him alone for a while so that he may think about the truth they had shared with him.

As the pilgrims enter a dark lane, they see a most fearful sight, a man whom seven devils had bound with seven cords being carried to the door in the side of the hill (the by-way to hell). On his back is a paper inscribed with the words "Wanton professor, and damnable Apostate." Those who live loosely may go merrily along, saying that they are more enlightened than others about God's great mercy and grace but forgetting the entangling tentacles of sin and how easy it is to be enslaved and ruined by a wanton spirit. Selfishness and carnal delights are not compatible with love for God and spiritual delights. Too soon sin will cause the warmth of love for God to cool, and we will fall into a cold, dead formalism resulting in hypocrisy and finally apostasy. The redeemed realize that there is no compatibility with the nature of Turn-away's profession if God has set up his kingdom in a heart, and they take from this a warning to examine their own lives.

Christian and Hopeful discuss the story of Little-Faith. How sad it is that this is a story that can be told of a great many Christians. We see that there are many Little-Faiths, who go doubting and trembling through life because they have been robbed of their assurance, peace, and joy (spending money). The robbery in the story would never have taken place if Little-Faith had been diligent in his pursuit of God. Instead he goes to sleep in Dead-man's lane, as relaxed and carefree as if he had already arrived at the end of his pilgrimage. When three rogues attack him, he is unable to ward them off, for his has been such a casual, comfortable journey thus far that he has never had to stretch and exercise his spiritual muscles by digging deep into God's Word or by spending a night in agonizing prayer. When disaster comes to believers whose spiritual muscles are flabby they are easily overcome, for they have no hidden life of prayer, Bible study, and communion with God by which to gain strength for the conflict.

Though the robbers took Little-Faith's spending money, they did not steal his jewels, for these are the graces by which a believer's soul is united to Christ (his adoption into God's family and Christ's robes of righteousness which have been bestowed on him by the Holy Spirit). Neither did they take his certificate, for this was a gift given by Christ and kept secure by him who is the author and finisher of the believer's faith. From the ineffectiveness of the church today we can see how often these same rogues must be attacking careless, weak believers. When difficult circumstances come, Mr. Faint-Heart kidnaps many believers, causing them to be discouraged and fearful; Mr. Mistrust holds hostage even more Christians trembling with doubts and lack of faith; and Mr. Guilt paralyzes pilgrims who continue to condemn themselves for past sins even though God, through Christ, has forgiven them. The efforts made to escape these rogues are feeble because of lack of knowledge and/or doubt of the Scriptures.

We witness the infinite goodness and mercy of God as these wicked men hear that Mr. Great Grace may be on the road and they flee. Little-Faith, robbed and wounded, spends the rest of his life begging, that is, riding on the coattails of other believers' experiences of joy, zeal, and knowledge. It is in this way, leaning on others, that he finishes his pilgrimage. Though Christians have no room to boast, for we are all rescued by grace, neither do we have to settle for second-hand notions of God by living on other believers' experiences.

Cheever says in defense of people like Little-Faith that after they have been robbed, "they go burdened with sin, and literally mourning after Christ, rather than believing in him. Yet, this mourning after Christ is something precious; it is infinitely better than hardness and indifference of heart, or false security, and infinitely better, also, than a dangerous, false confidence, or a joy that has not a scriptural foundation. Little-Faith had a tender conscience, which made him bewail his sinful sleep, and all his failings by the way" (*Lectures on the Pilgrim's Progress*, p. 437). Little-Faith had a weak faith, but it was a real faith, for he had no trust in his own merits at all and it is better to have little faith, even with the lack of comfort and joy, than to have none at all.

From this story we learn that Christians should always be striving earnestly to grow in the grace and knowledge of our Lord Jesus Christ. For when we become content with just a little bit of Christianity, we are opening ourselves up to be robbed of our joy, assurance, and strength. As Cheever also points out concerning this story:

> Hopeful seemed to think if he had been in Little-Faith's place, he would not have given up so easily; but Christian bade him beware of self-confidence, for it was a very different thing to hear of these villains who attacked Little-Faith, and to be attacked by them oneself. . . . Peter once thought he would never give up; he was ready to try what he could do even to go to prison and to death, but when these grim robbers came upon him, "though some do say that he is the Prince of the Apostles, they handled him so, that they made him at last afraid of a sorry girl." So there is no help, trust, strength, or safety for us but in Christ, in his great grace in us, upon us, and for us. Great-Grace must be our champion, as he was Little-Faith's or it is all over with us. (Ibid., pp. 438–39)

Our reliance for salvation and victory in spiritual conflicts is on the grace of God exhibited in Christ's atoning sacrifice and applied to his people. May we always be making use of the means of grace for our spiritual growth but ever clinging to Christ, for he is our only desire and sure hope.

After dealing quite triumphantly, in their opinion, with Little-Faith, haughty Christian and Hopeful continue on their way. This attitude of superiority to weak Christians quickly leads to a bad situation for both of them. Not only should they have remembered Christ's statement that he would not break the bruised reed nor quench the smoking flax, but their high-mindedness causes them to lean to their own (as they suppose superior) knowledge and choose a way that seems to lie as straight as the way by which they should go. This choice is made without consulting Scripture and without prayer; instead, a cunning method is employed by Satan to cause them harm. Flattery can be a dangerous enemy to the heart and mind. Disguising itself as praise for truly good attainments in Christian growth, it subtly leads to spiritual pride when one takes all the credit, forgetting the enabling power of the Holy Spirit in all that has eternal worth. An overinflated ego can quickly become self-sufficient, so that rather than trusting at all times in Christ, the believer makes choices on the basis of his or her own inclinations and interests. Beware of any who would cause you to take your eyes off Jesus and place them on yourself. This black figure clothed in white is the white devil of self-righteousness and is more dangerous than the black devil of open sin. Luther said, "You need not fear a black devil half so much as a white one" (Spurgeon, *Pictures from Pilgrim's Progress*, p. 175). The Flatterer does not tell them to forsake Christ directly, for they would have rejected that deliberate sin right away; instead he deludes them into thinking that now that they have learned so much from the shepherds, they are able to make a few decisions on their own. Why bother praying or looking at Scripture for guidance about such a small decision, which they are now perfectly able to make on their own? We see that by small degrees the pilgrims' faces are turned away from Christ and the correct path and that they are soon entangled in the net of their own prideful error.

A Shining One then comes to their rescue. This Shining One is meant to represent the Holy Spirit who is the leader and guide for all believers. When Christians stray from Jesus, who is the Way, the Truth, and the Life, the Holy Spirit comes with his rod of conviction and chastisement to whip them from their prideful folly back to relying wholly and humbly on Christ.

Christian and Hopeful go softly along the Way until they meet a man with his back towards Zion, whose name is Atheist. How numerous are the enemies of Christ, for no sooner do the pilgrims escape the self-righteous Flatterer than they must deal with a profane mocker who openly sets himself against all religion! His twenty-year search has yielded him nothing, which is not surprising since he has searched with a worldly heart and a dead faith. Even if he had found the Celestial City and been able to enter it, he would not have enjoyed it for a moment, for one must have a new heart and be a new creature in Christ in order to enjoy heaven. What had been pointed out to him on the road of the pilgrim was the sin in his life, which was enough to make him want to desert the Way and all that goes with it rather than face his sin, forsake it, and flee to Christ. How sad it is that he thinks he can refresh himself with the temporal things of this world, which he had once cast away! When tempted to disbelief, we should do as Christian and Hopeful do; remember past visions of Mount Zion (lean on past experiences of God's deliverance) and remember corrections for past mistakes (e.g., the chastisement of the Shining One).

We now come to the part of the journey which is the most dangerous, for more seeming pilgrims have been destroyed here than have been destroyed by lions, dragons, or giants. The enchanted ground lulls many a drowsy soul to sleep, for when things go easily, smoothly, and well, one is more apt to be less attentive in the ways of the Lord and to cease watching against sin. The world, the flesh, and the Devil have the same pull as gravity on our souls, always down. Pilgrims are liable to become weary with the struggle towards the end of their journey, and this is why the enchanted ground is placed so near to the borders of the Celestial City. Sleep is good for the physical body, but for the soul it can be deadly. Let us turn to Spurgeon now to answer the question. What is it to take a nap in religion?

> Slumbering Christian, behold a picture of your condition. Have you not sometimes mourned your insensibility? You wished you could feel; but all you felt was pain because you could not feel. . . . You go to the house of God; but when the multitude in the full tide of song send their music up to Heaven, you hear it, but your heart does not leap at the sound. Prayer goeth solemnly up to God's throne, like the smoke of the evening sacrifice; once, you could pray, too; but, now, while your body is in the house of God, your heart is elsewhere. You have become like a formalist; you feel that there is not the savor, that unction, in the preaching, that there used to be. There is no difference in your minister, you know; the change is in yourself. The hymns and the prayers are just the same, but you have fallen into a state of slumber. . . . Why are the prayer-meetings almost universally neglected? Where is the spirit of prayer, where the life of devotion? Is it not almost extinct? . . . This is not the sleep of Jacob, in which a ladder unites Heaven and earth, and angels tread the ascending rounds; but this is the sleep in which ladders are raised from hell, and devils climb upward from the pit to seize thy slumbering spirit. Sleepy Christian, let me shout in thine ears,—thou art sleeping while souls are being lost,—sleeping while men are being damned,—sleeping while hell is being peopled,—sleeping while Christ is being dishonored,—while the devil is grinning at thy sleepy face,—

sleeping while demons are dancing round thy slumbering carcass, and telling it in hell that a Christian is asleep. (*Pictures from Pilgrim's Progress*, pp. 183–87)

So we are instructed that while we pilgrims sleep, demons snatch our eternal treasures, but we do not see them; hell's fire burns hot but we do not feel it, nor do we smell the burning flesh of its inhabitants; the minister cries a warning, but we do not hear it, nor do we hear the laughter of the demons at our folly. Sleepy pilgrims remember the shepherd's warning: do not sleep on the enchanted ground—not even a short nap!

How are we to be kept from this slumber (i.e., lukewarm formality in worship, spiritual coldness in prayer and Bible reading, and hearts shut to a vivid view of spiritual realities)? Pray to God that it may be as it was with Christian and Hopeful, who "managed well" by fellowship rather than by affliction and persecution. Certainly troubles make us watchful, and a distressed soul does not sleep, but all would agree that lively conversation about the ways of the Lord is much to be preferred.

Hopeful tells Christian of his own Christian experience and his conversion. In this conversation we are shown God's mercy and grace in the way he had dealt with Hopeful in bringing him to conviction, repentance, and conversion. Hopeful had tried to shut his eyes and resist God's gracious dealings with him in convicting him of his sin, but we can be thankful that God's drawing him to Christ could not be resisted. In Hopeful's account of his conversion is demonstrated the fact that God is sovereign in bestowing salvation. Natural man is dead (spiritually) in his trespasses and sins (Ephesians 2:1). Just as a physically dead man cannot hear or see, so the spiritually dead man cannot see or comprehend the things of God (John 3:3–9). Unless the Spirit gives life (regeneration) no one is able to exercise faith in Christ—"The Spirit gives life; the flesh counts for nothing" (John 6:63, NIV). Not only are people dead when it comes to spiritual matters, they are totally averse to God: "The mind set on the flesh is hostile toward God; for it does not subject itself to the law of God, for it is not even able to do so" (Romans 8:7). No one will seek God unless God draws that person—"No one can come to Me [Christ], unless the Father who sent Me draws him" (John 6:44)—for the Bible states that "there is *none righteous*, not even one; there is *none who understands*, there is *none who seeks* for God" (Romans 3:10, 11, emphasis added). Human nature and God's grace are two direct opposites. The carnal nature opposes grace, but grace subdues nature and brings it to submission. Faith is a gift given by God (Ephesians 2:8, 9) and when the Holy Spirit gives life, we then become willing and able to reach out and accept Christ. Those who teach that unbelievers can believe at any time by their own power apart from the Holy Spirit's regeneration are saying the exact opposite of what Scripture says, for John 6:65 states, "No one can come to Me, unless it has been granted him from the Father"; and "When the Gentiles heard this, they began rejoicing and glorifying the word of the Lord; and as many as had been appointed to eternal life believed" (Acts 13:48). It is sad that the majority of evangelical pulpits today assert that faith precedes regeneration. The great Reformers Martin Luther and John Calvin both taught the inability of man and the sovereign grace of God in salvation. Let us not go back to pre-Reformation times, when the teaching of the church was that God and man co-operate in salvation (synergism), but let us stand with the men of the Reformation and declare that it is God and God alone who saves (monergism). Not unto us, O Lord, be the glory, but unto thy name be all the glory.

Many of us can identify with Hopeful concerning the hours of conviction during which his sins would be brought to his mind by his hearing the Bible being read or, by the example of a godly believer, such as the time when the death of a friend made him view his own death and then the judgment. This caused Hopeful to attempt to live a good life by forsaking his sin and his sinful friends and, by praying, reading the Bible, etc. But trouble came tumbling upon him in spite of his reformation, as he learned that "by the works of the Law shall no man be justified." Even if he were able to keep the Law perfectly, this would not remove the debt he owed for past sins. Hopeful realized that if he was to stand before a holy, just God he could not stand on his own merit but must have the perfect righteousness of Christ. Faithful told him that he needed the righteousness of a man who has never sinned credited to his account and directed him to the mercy seat to plead with God "to make him know and believe in Jesus Christ."

How different is the God-centered gospel presented in this section from today's distorted, watered-down version! In today's man-centered gospel we hear much about the love of God but little about his holiness—but holiness and love are equally important attributes of God. This unbalanced emphasis on God's love detracts from the sense of sinfulness in offending a holy, just God who does not let the guilty go unpunished (Exodus 34:7). The easy believism of today says that submitting to Christ's lordship is an optional part of salvation. However, Scripture teaches that an attitude of submission to Christ's lordship is necessary for salvation (Matthew 7:21–23). A commitment to Christ is not only a mental assent to the truths of the gospel message—even the demons do that (James 2:19)—but also a response of the whole person (mind, heart, and will) leading to a holy life and a desire to please God and give him honor and glory in all that one does. It is God's choice of us before the foundation of the world (Ephesians 1:4) that is the basis of our salvation, and we respond to his gracious choice and invitation. And so Hopeful prayed, pleaded, and waited on God, hoping that he might be gracious to him, an undeserving sinner.

The effect the revelation of Christ had on Hopeful's soul is beautifully described in the story of how he was brought to understand the nature of justifying faith and the beauty of Christ. He was so overwhelmed that his response was "love to the name, people, and ways of Jesus Christ," and if he had had a thousand gallons of blood in his body, he could have spilled it all for the sake of the Lord Jesus.

L·E·S·S·O·N

10

Ignorance Dismisses Christian's Gospel

Barbour and Company, Inc. 1985, pp. 165–78
Discovery House *New Pilgrim's Progress* with notes, pp. 169–81
Moody *Pilgrim's Progress in Today's English*, pp. 138–47
Moody Classic Edition, pp. 167–79
Revell Spire Book, pp. 135–45
Whitaker House 1981 Edition, pp. 174–87

Questions for Discussion or Reflection

In this section Christian and Hopeful have another encounter and discourse with Ignorance. Ignorance reveals his blindness to the corruption of his own heart and his vain confidence in himself instead of complete reliance on Christ's active and passive obedience for pardon and justification. After speaking to Ignorance about salvation and pressing him to trust Christ, Christian and Hopeful leave him to himself and continue their journey. A profitable conversation ensues about the way in which God uses conviction of sin and the punishment due sin to direct sinners to the cross. Next the pilgrims discuss an acquaintance of theirs who became a backslider because he was a total stranger to his own heart, the truths of God's laws, and the glorious gospel.

1. As Christian and Hopeful continue to walk through the enchanted ground, they notice Ignorance behind them. They wait for him to catch

up with them so that they may talk with him further about the gospel. On what basis does Ignorance hope that all stands well between God and his soul?

2. Ignorance's hope is based ultimately on one authority, his heart. What does Christian say should be his authority instead?

3. What did Christian say that "the Word of God saith of persons in a Natural Condition"?

4. Ignorance asks, "What are good thoughts of God?" How does Christian respond?

5. What is Ignorance's definition of justification, which differs from the Protestant definition and is similar to that of Catholicism?

6. Christian gives a four point correction to Ignorance's confession of faith. What are the four points?

7. How does Ignorance respond to Christian?

8. How does Christian answer Ignorance's incorrect conclusion?

9. Christian and Hopeful have a discussion about the role of fear in leading a person to Christ. How does Christian describe the right kind of fear?

How do ignorant men try to stifle convictions that make them fear?

10. Christian and Hopeful now discuss a man who "dwelt in Grace-less, a town about two miles off of Honesty, and he dwelt next door to one Turnback." Who was he, and what reasons are given for his sudden backsliding?

Christian gives an illustration of an incomplete repentance. What is it?

Christian lists nine steps in backsliding. Were any of these warning signs to you? Which ones particularly?

Note: Rev. John Gulliver has these comments on how to prevent back-sliding:

> It begins in the unbelief of the heart, and ends in open sins in the life. Why is the love of this world so forbidden? Why is covetousness called idolatry? Because whatever draws away the heart from God, and prevents enjoying close fel-lowship with him, naturally tends to apostasy from him. Look well to your hearts and affections. Daily learn to obey that command, "Keep thy heart with all diligence, for out of it are the issues of life." Proverbs 4:23. If you neglect to watch, you will be sure to smart under the sense of sin on earth or its curse in hell. (*The Complete Works of John Bunyan*, pp. 165–66)

Summary and Applications

The pilgrims have another conference with Ignorance.

Hopeful's experience stands in a fine instructive contrast with that of Ignorance; the first shows the relish of the renewed heart for pure divine truth, and the secret of it; the second shows the secret of the opposition of the unrenewed heart against that same divine truth in its purity. The pride of our nature is one of the last evils revealed to ourselves, and whatever goes against it, we do naturally count as our enemy. But humility, learning of Christ, makes a different estimate, and counts as precious, beyond price, all that truth and virtue in the gospel which abases self. On the other hand, those who do not love God cannot expect to find in his Word a system of truth that will please their own hearts. A sinful heart can have no right views of God, and of course will have defective views of his Word; for sin distorts the judgment, and overturns the balance of the mind on all moral subjects far more than even the best of men are aware of. There is, there can be, no true reflection of God or of his Word from the bosom darkened with guilt, from the heart at enmity with him. That man will always look at God through the medium of his own selfishness, and at God's Word through the coloring of his own wishes, prejudices, and fears. (Cheever, *Lectures on the Pilgrim's Progress*, pp. 446–47)

Thus, Ignorance because of his pride and self-righteousness is a stranger to his own wicked heart and is deceived into vain confidence. "As long as men will continue to look at God's truth through the medium of their own pride and prejudice, so long they will have mistaken views of God and eternity, so long will their own self-righteousness look better to them for a resting place than the glorious righteousness of Him, who of God is made unto us our wisdom, righteousness, sanctification and redemption" (ibid., p. 448). Though God's truth is clear, Ignorance's depraved mind dims and distorts this truth and makes a religious system in which he cooperates (by his works) with Christ for his right standing with God. Ignorance has made Christ a justifier of his religious duties instead of trusting in Christ wholly and solely for acceptance before God. Believers, because of their love for divine teachings, understand that they may glory in nothing in and of themselves concerning their salvation but only in Christ and what he has done in and for them. So Ignorance is to be an object of pity because of his boastfulness, which is a sign of his great delusion.

Ignorance is so dismayed by Christian's statement that Christ's righteousness alone is the believer's justification that he declares that this belief system will lead to antinomianism (lawlessness). However, believers, who have had Christ revealed to them through the Word, realize the true fullness of the gospel (that our salvation is totally, from beginning to end, all of Christ) and will have such love and gratitude that they will want to obey the Law. Unless God is pleased to reveal Christ and the gospel (Matthew 11:27) to Ignorance, he will forever be captive to his notions of works salvation, though Ignorance is himself responsible for his sinful blindness.

After slighting Christian and Hopeful's good counsel, Ignorance hobbles behind them because of his self-conceit and pride. Our pilgrims have a discussion about how the fear of the Lord is the beginning of wisdom. God uses fear of the consequences of sin to cause people to examine themselves, and if it is to be a profitable examination, it must be done by the light of Scripture. The right kind of fear, which God uses for good, may be distinguished by its origin (God's special grace), and it results in a person's depending totally on Christ for salvation. It produces and maintains within the soul a deep reverence for God, his Word, and his ways, keeping the heart sensitive and making it hesitant to turn from what is pleasing to God. Godly fear keeps a soul humble and dependent on the Holy Spirit to enable holy living, therefore, the person who has this fear desires not to grieve the Holy Spirit. Love and gratitude come from the knowledge of God's great mercy and grace exhibited in the gospel; thus, the one who has this knowledge desires fellowship and communion with God above any delights that sin may bring. A Christian will not want to do anything that might bring dishonor to God or give an enemy reason to speak scornfully of God or his kingdom.

People seek to stifle conviction of sin by thinking that it comes from the Devil; this spoils their supposed faith, and thus they become presumptuously confident. They believe that fears of sin's consequences take away from their self-holiness. The personal righteousness they claim is one that comes from the natural man (his supposed good heart) and causes them to applaud and be confident in themselves instead of desiring and trusting in Christ's righteousness. Such presumption in the unbeliever is fatal.

Hopeful admits that he had engaged in the same incorrect thinking before God graciously enlightened his mind and opened his eyes to the truth. It is good to look back at our condition before conversion, for it causes us to be thankful to God because it is his mercy and grace only that have made us different from those who are living in the delusion of pride and self-righteousness, whom we should only pity.

The conversation next turns to Temporary, who dwelt in the town of Graceless. Hopeful draws on his acquaintance with Temporary to set forth several reasons (taken from his own observation of backsliders) why so many people's religion is such a temporary thing, why so many run well for a time, and then stand still, and then turn back. He describes them as having a conscience alarmed at the consequences of sin; but when guilt wears off, they go back to their old ways. They have a desire for religion because they don't want hell, not because their hearts have been changed to love God and have a desire to be with him. And when they meet Shame, she is easily able to talk them into renouncing their profession of faith. "So deceitful is the human heart that you could not believe what compelling reasons such a mean-spirited man will face you with as to why he should leave all the ways he once so delighted in for a piece of bread, and for the smile of the open enemies of his church, his faith, and the Savior" (Whyte, *Second Series Bunyan Characters*, p. 59). For such that are like Temporary, the root of the matter is that they have not searched their own hearts to see the evil in them. They have conviction of sin but it is not complete or deep enough. Nor has sin become really bitter to the inner man. Thomas Shepherd cautions: "Be sure your wound for sin at first is deep enough. For all the error in a man's faith and sanctification springs from his first error in his humiliation. If a man's humiliation be false, or even weak or little, then his faith and his hold of Christ are weak and little, and his sanctification counterfeit. But if a man's wound be right, and his humiliations deep enough, that man's faith will be right and his sanctification will be glorious" (Shepard, *The Parable of the Ten Virgins*, p. 482). So we learn that if people see little sin in their heart, then their esteem of Christ's work on the cross will be little, and there will also be little love of the Savior. Temporaries are not dead to every hope of saving themselves, although they do not realize their hopeless situation apart from Christ. They have indeed been alarmed, but terror without humiliation will never subvert self-confidence, and they will always be ready to turn back to the world at an expedient time.

Pilgrims on the Way should take from the character of Temporary a warning to examine their hearts, for all backsliding begins in the heart, the seat of our affections. When we neglect prayer and our Bibles and are preoccupied with the pursuit of the things of this world (fame, material goods, pleasure, etc.), it is a sure indication that our affections are going astray and becoming lukewarm towards God. We should daily follow the command, "Keep thy heart with all diligence; for out of it are the issues of life" (Proverbs 4:23, KJV). A Christian should diligently make use of the means of grace to keep fuel in the heart that it may burn hot in its affections toward God. We should be forever pressing toward the mark of our high calling in Christ, for to stand still is to go back, which we do all too easily. This idea can be illustrated by the image of a Christian going up a down escalator. If the believer should cease to vigorously climb upward for a minute, he or she will lose ground, and be carried downward.

L·E·S·S·O·N
11
Christian Reaches the Celestial City

Barbour and Company, Inc. 1985, pp. 178–90
Discovery House *New Pilgrim's Progress* with notes, pp. 181–92
Moody *Pilgrim's Progress in Today's English*, pp. 149–56
Moody Classic Edition, pp. 179–91
Revell Spire Book, pp. 145–54
Whitaker House 1981 Edition, pp. 188–99

Questions for Discussion or Reflection

In this, our last lesson, we reach the end of the journey with Christian and Hopeful. Upon entering into the Country of Beulah, "Christian with desire fell sick," and "Hopeful also had a fit or two of the same disease." After being refreshed by the dainties of this land, the pilgrims sleep and then prepare to cross over the river of Death, their last enemy. Looking unto Jesus, the author and finisher of their faith (Hebrews 12:1), they arrive on the other side of the river. At the Lord's command the gate of glory is opened to them and they are admitted to the glorious city. We take one last look at the awful delusion of Ignorance, whereby we may assess our own hope to find out whether it is a vain hope or a hope founded only upon our union with Christ, who is the Way, the Truth, and the Life.

1. As the pilgrims continue on the Way, they enter the Country of Beulah. Beulah means "married"; the name is taken from Isaiah 62.

What part of the Christian's pilgrimage do you think the country of Beulah represents?

2. Christian and Hopeful must cross a river before they can arrive at the gate to the Celestial City. Describe how each man crosses this river.

3. Why are the pilgrims able to go up the mighty hill on which the city stands with ease?

4. What do the Shining Ones tell the pilgrims about the glory of the city?

When Christian and Hopeful ask, "What must we do in the Holy Place?" what do the Shining Ones tell them?

5. What type of welcome are Christian and Hopeful given as they draw near the gate?

6. What things do Christian and Hopeful present to the men at the gate, which are carried to the King?

7. Why is Ignorance able to cross the river "without half the difficulty which the other two men met with"?

What happens to Ignorance at the gate of the city?

We have read previously that Ignorance relied on what to gain entrance into the city?

8. In the conclusion, what warnings are given?

What exhortations are given?

Summary and Applications

Christian and Hopeful enter the country of Beulah. This land is meant to represent the sweet peace and confidence that believers should experience towards the close of their lives. It is the soul that is spiritually minded and living on the borders of heaven. Here Christians have visions of eternity, believers' hearts long to be with the lover of their souls and desire to be free from the sin that continually tries to entrap them, and pilgrims anticipate delightful fellowship with the saints in heaven. Here also "the contract between the Bride and the Bridegroom was renewed." Oh, sweet contract, our engagement day, when we first accepted Christ's proposal to make us his bride. Better still is the believer's dying, for surely this is our wedding day, when Christ will lift the veil from his bride's face, and as the veil is lifted, we shall see our beloved clearly for the first time.

After a delightful stay in the country of Beulah the pilgrims proceed towards the Celestial City. Two men approach and tell them that they must still meet with two more difficulties. We learn that these difficulties are death without and unbelief within. The unbelief within is what makes death distressing to us. The Puritans had a lifelong concern about preparing for death and dying well. Bunyan wrote, "Consider thou must die but once; I mean as to this world, for if thou, when thou goest hence, dost not die well, thou canst not come back again and die better" (Offor, *The Works of John Bunyan*, 1:686).

So finally the pilgrims meet their last enemy, death. When death stares them in the face, their fears arise, but through the river they must go. What are they to look at? Certainly not at themselves, at what they have done and been. No, they must look only to Jesus, who has conquered death for his redeemed children and can and will overcome the fear of death in them. Faith in Jesus and in what he has done for them supplies the solid ground they need to walk on in order to pass through the river of death.

> O children of God! death hath lost its sting, because the devil's power over it is destroyed. Then cease to fear dying. Thou knowest what death is: look him in the face, and tell him thou art not afraid of him. Ask grace from God, that by an intimate knowledge and firm belief of thy Master's death, thou mayest be strengthened for that dread hour. And mark me, if thou so livest, thou mayest be able to think of death with pleasure, and to welcome it when it comes with intense delight. It is sweet to die: to lie upon the breast of Christ, and have one's soul kissed out of one's body by the lips of divine affection. (Spurgeon, *The New Park Street Pulpit*, 4:15)

For the Christian's soul, death is her lover's kiss.

Cheever speaks of death as God's messenger to bring his children home:

> There are souls that welcome him [death], for he opens the prison door, out of which they are to pass into a world of light; out of a prison of flesh, sin, fear, doubt and bondage, into a celestial freedom in the perfection of holiness; into love, praise, and blissful adoration, without any mixture of sin, any cloud or shadow of defilement, or any thing for ever and ever to mar or change the perfect peace and blessedness of the soul. To such souls, death is but the messenger, to take them before the throne of God in his likeness, to present them without spot, or wrinkle or any such thing. Death is Life to such; it is the being born out of a state of sinfulness, darkness, and wretchedness in fallen humanity, into a condition of purity, light, and happiness, in a city where the glory of God doth lighten it, and the Lamb is the light thereof. There is no future terror, of which Death is King, in such a

case. Dying is but going home. (*Lectures on the Pilgrim's Progress*, pp. 462–63)

Christians should look at death with the sure hope that they go to their eternal home of glory. What will be the first words you will say to Jesus as he opens the door and you arrive home at last?

Bunyan, in describing the path from the river of death to the gate, has done

what no other devout writer . . . has ever done; he has filled what perhaps in most minds is a mere blank, a vacancy, or at most a bewilderment and mist of glory, with definite and beatific images, with natural thoughts, and with sympathizing communion of gentle spirits, who form, as it were, an outer porch and perspective of glory, through which the soul passes into uncreated light. Bunyan has thrown a bridge, as it were, for the imagination, over the deep, sudden, open space of an untried spiritual existence; where it finds, ready to receive the soul that leaves the body, ministering spirits, sent forth to minister unto them who are to be heirs of salvation. (Ibid., p. 456)

Even considering such a magnificent account, it is to be wondered what amazing marvels Bunyan would share were he to come back and give a description of what he has experienced and seen since his death. "Eye hath not seen, nor ear heard, neither have entered into the heart of man, the things which God hath prepared for them that love him" (1 Corinthians 2:9, KJV).

After lifting us up to the very heights of heaven, Bunyan then brings us to a very solemn and instructive portion of the story as he shows us what becomes of Ignorance. Vain-Hope had been Ignorance's companion all his life and he did not desert him at death. Ignorance had set out on his journey relying on his own presumed righteousness, and God had given him over to this evil, satanic delusion and left him to perish in this lie. Of such a deluded believer's funeral Spurgeon writes:

At the head of the mournful cavalcade is Beelzebub, leading the procession, and, looking back with twinkling eye, and leer of malicious joy, says, "Here is fine pomp to conduct a soul to hell with!" Ah! plumes and hearse for the man who is being conducted to his last abode in hell! A string of carriages to do honor to the man whom God has cursed in life and cursed in death; for the hope of the hypocrite is evermore in an accursed one. And a bell is ringing, and the clergyman is reading the funeral service, and is burying the man "in sure and certain hope." Oh! what a laugh rings up from somewhere a little lower down than the grave! "In sure and certain hope," says Satan; "ha! ha! your sure and certain hope is folly indeed. Trust to a bubble, and hope to fly to the stars; trust to the wild winds, that they shall conduct you safely to heaven; but trust to such as that, and thou art a madman indeed." (*New Park Street Pulpit*, 4:284–85)

And so Ignorance, who had been instructed by Christian and Hopeful that the righteousness of Christ is the only hope for sinful man, trusts in his own works and deeds and crosses the river of death on the boat belonging to Vain-Hope.

Finally our dreamer describes the end of Ignorance, how he is bound and carried to the door in the side of the hill. The dreamer says, "Then I saw that there was a Way to Hell, even from the gates of Heaven, as well as from the City of Destruction." A very somber conclusion to his dream indeed. Gulliver asks us to take this final exam in view of the lessons we have learned:

Consider deeply. Weigh attentively, so as to get good satisfaction from the word, to these important questions: Am I in Christ *the way*, the only way to the kingdom, or not? Do I see that all other ways, whether of sin or self-righteousness, lead to hell? Does Christ dwell in my heart by faith? Am I a new creature in him? Do I renounce my own righteousness, as well as abhor my sins? Do I look to Christ alone for mercy, and depend only on him for holiness? Is he the only hope of my soul, and the only confidence of my heart? And do I desire to be found in him, knowing by the Word, and feeling by the teaching of his Spirit, that I am totally lost in myself? Thus is Christ formed in me, the only hope of glory? Do I study to please him, as well as hope to enjoy him? Is fellowship with God the Father, and his Son Jesus Christ, so prized by me, as to seek it and esteem it above all things? If so, though I may find all

things in nature, in the world, and from Satan, continually op-
posing this, yet I am in Christ *the way*, and he is in me *the truth*
and *the life*. I am one with him, and he is one with me. (*The
Complete Works of John Bunyan*, pp. 170–71)

Rock of Ages, cleft for me, let me hide myself in thee;
Let the water and the blood, from thy riven side which flowed,
Be of sin the double cure, cleanse me from its guilt and pow'r.

Not the labors of my hands can fulfill thy law's demands;
Could my zeal no respite know, could my tears forever flow,
All for sin could not atone; thou must save, and thou alone.

Nothing in my hand I bring, simply to thy cross I cling;
Naked, come to thee for dress; helpless, look to thee for grace;
Foul, I to the Fountain fly; wash me, Savior, or I die.

While I draw this fleeting breath, when mine eyelids close in
    death,
When I soar to worlds unknown, see thee on thy judgment
    throne,
Rock of Ages, cleft for me, let me hide myself in thee.

(Augustus M. Toplady, 1776)

Bibliography of Works Cited

Bunyan, John. *Grace Abounding to the Chief of Sinners.* 3d ed. Hertfordshire: Evangelical Press, 1988.

————. *The Pilgrim's Progress.* Uhrichsville, Ohio: Barbour, 1985.

Cheever, George. *Lectures on the Pilgrim's Progress, and on the Life and Times of John Bunyan.* New York: Robert Carter & Brothers, 1875.

Edwards, Jonathan. *The Works of Jonathan Edwards with a memoir by Sereno E. Dwight revised and corrected by Edward Hickman.* 5th ed. 2 vols. Edinburgh; Carlisle: Banner of Truth, 1988.

Gulliver, John. *The Complete Works of John Bunyan with introduction and comments by Rev. John P. Gulliver, D.D.* Philadelphia: William Garretson & Co., 1872.

Kuiper, R. B. *The Glorious Body of Christ.* 3d ed. Edinburgh; Carlisle: Banner of Truth, 1987.

Offor, George, ed. *The Works of John Bunyan.* 3 vols. Edinburgh; Carlisle: Banner of Truth, 1991.

Ryle, J. C. *Holiness, Its Nature, Hindrances, Difficulties, and Roots.* Cambridge; London: James Clarke & Co., 1956.

Scott, Thomas. *The Pilgrim's Progress by John Bunyan with Explanatory Notes by Thomas Scott.* Sterling: Grace Abounding Ministries, 1986.

Shepard, Thomas. *The Parable of the Ten Virgins.* Ligonier: Soli Deo Gloria, 1990.

Spurgeon, Charles. *The Metropolitan Tabernacle,* 56 vols. Pasadena: Pilgrim, 1975.

————. *The New Park Street Pulpit.* 6 vols. Grand Rapids: Baker, 1990.

————. *Pictures from Pilgrim's Progress.* Pasadena: Pilgrim, 1992.

Webster's Eighth New Collegiate Dictionary. Springfield, Mass: G. & C. Merriam Company, 1979.

Whyte, Alexander. *First Series Bunyan Characters Lectures Delivered in St. George's Free Church Edinburgh*. 2d ed. Edinburgh; London: Oliphant Anderson and Ferrier, 1895.

————. *Second Series Bunyan Characters Lectures Delivered in St. George's Free Church Edinburgh*. Edinburgh; London: Oliphant Anderson and Ferrier, 1894.